U0503232

帝国余晖
中古国藏晚清官窑瓷器

主编
杨静荣 张崇檀

文物出版社

2011年

CHINA ANCIENT
ARTS & CRAFT
INTERNATIONAL
中古陶

杨静荣 ◇ Yang Jingrong

　　1948 年生于北京，北京故宫博物院研究员，复旦大学历史系毕业，曾在邯郸陶瓷研究所从事陶瓷颜料和传统色釉的研究实验工作，1979 年调入故宫博物院研究陶瓷史至今。1976 年在《文物》杂志发表第一篇论文《漫谈我国古代的花釉工艺》，至今发表论文近百篇，与他人合著出版专著《中国的陶瓷》、《中国陶瓷》、《民间陶瓷》、《龙与中国文化》4 部。个人独立专著已出版《颜色釉》、《古陶瓷鉴识》、《颜色釉陶瓷的鉴赏和鉴定》、《龙之源》。

张崇檀 ◇ Zhang Chongtan

中古陶（北京）国际艺术品有限公司执行董事、总经理、中古陶（北京）艺术品投资管理有限公司董事长、北京中陶古艺术品鉴定技术开发中心总经理、文化部艺术品评估委员会科技检测委员会副主任。

1962 年 10 月出生于山东龙口。1983 年毕业于黑龙江大学法律专业；2007 届北大资源学院陶瓷鉴定专业本科毕业；2010 年中央民族大学民族学文物鉴定方向研究生毕业。

自 2002 年至今，陆续在北京创办了北京中陶古艺术品鉴定技术开发中心、中古陶（北京）国际艺术品有限公司、中古陶（北京）艺术品投资管理有限公司等集鉴定、交易、投资管理为一体的艺术品经营管理机构。由于其在文物科技鉴定技术开发与市场运用方面的突出贡献，于 2006 年受聘于文化部艺术评估委员会担任科技检测委员会副主任一职。在经营管理中陶、中古陶企业 9 年过程中，探讨摸索出一套成功的"双轨制"鉴定方法，是在中国文物艺术品鉴定交易行业提出"保真交易"并赋予实施的第一人。2008 年被评为北青网文化创意产业 108 将，同时《北京青年周刊》发表《张崇檀·有创新就有活力》专栏文章，2010 年北京电视台科技频道以《法眼识真——张崇檀》、2011 年《北京日报》以《文物诚可贵，真话价更高》为题进行专题报道。主要文章有《试论"双轨制"鉴定方法在文物鉴定领域中的应用》、《双轨制文物艺术品鉴定方法在规避文物艺术品投资风险中的作用》等，与杨静荣、古方合著有《汝窑瓷器鉴赏》、《汉代夔龙凤鸟纹玉璧的用途及意义》等。

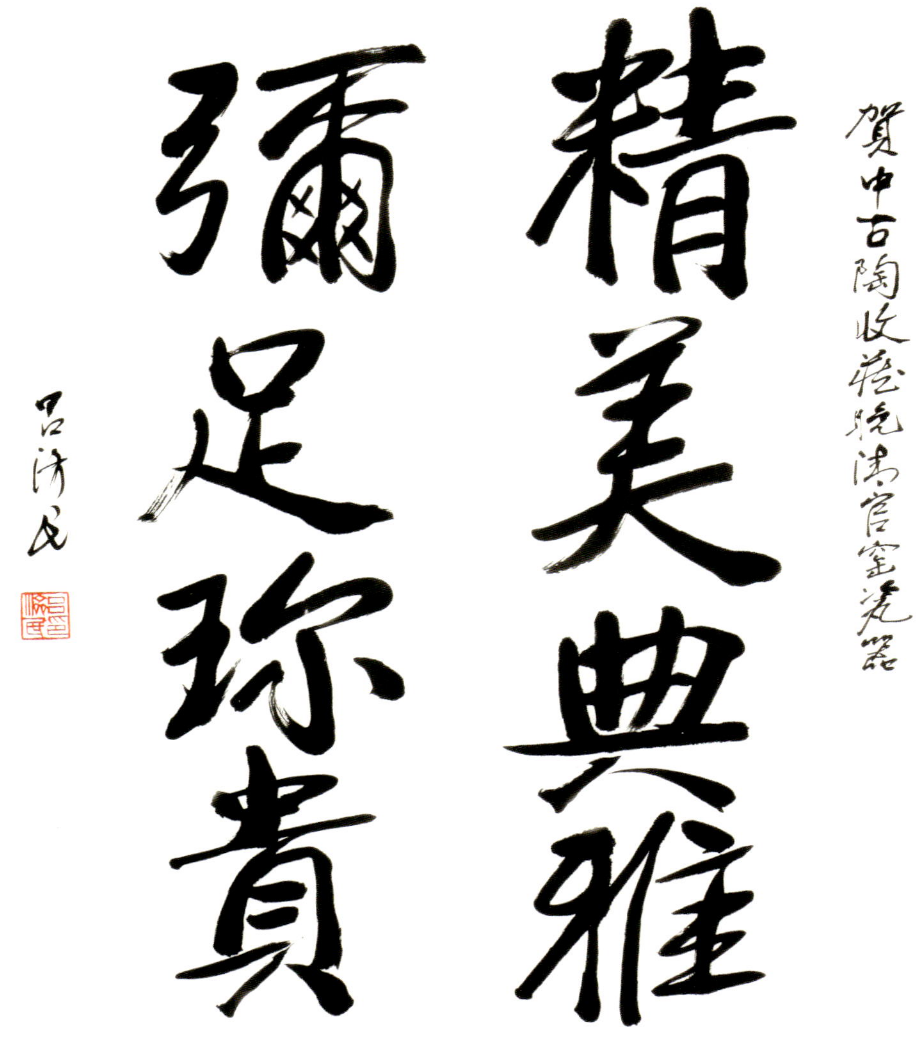

精美典雅
彌足珍貴

贺中古陶收藏院满官窑瓷器

吕济民

吕济民

国家文物局原局长、故宫博物院原院长

现任国家文物局博物馆专家组组长、故宫博物院研究员

北京文物局博物馆专家组组长

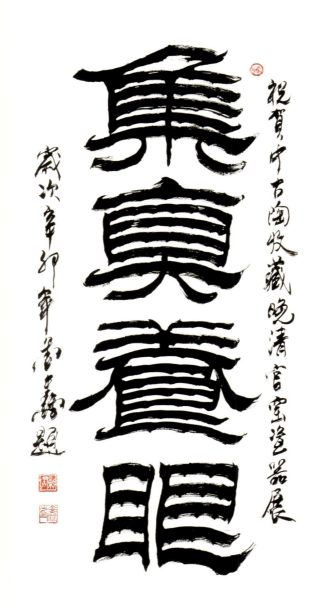

集真鉴眼

祝贺中古陶收藏晚清官窑瓷器展

岁次辛卯仲冬金鑫题

金鑫

书画鉴定专家、书法家
中古陶（北京）国际艺术品有限公司艺术总监
中古陶（北京）艺术品投资管理有限公司艺术总监

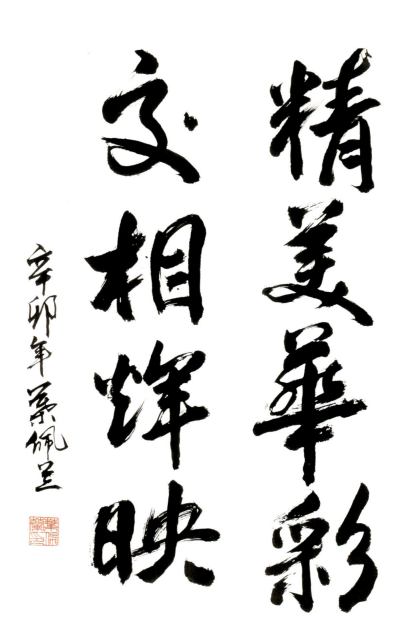

精美華彩　文相輝映

辛卯年 葉佩蘭

叶佩兰

故宫博物院研究员

中国文物学会常务理事

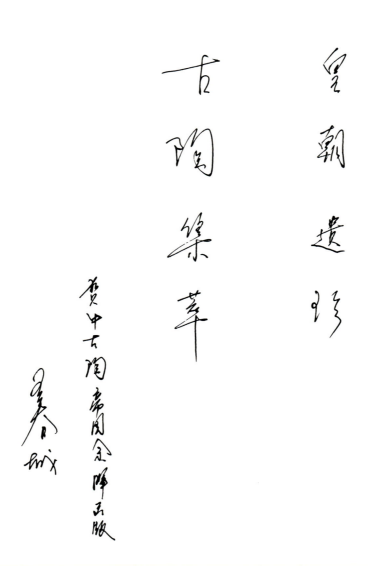

皇朝遗珍

古陶集萃

贺中古陶鸾陶金牌玉版

春城

王春城

首都博物馆研究员．文物资源调查征集部主任
北京市文物鉴定委员会委员

北京市文物鉴定委员会

中古陶（北京）国际艺术品有限公司所
藏晚清官窑瓷器，实属难得，展现了晚
清瓷器的工艺水平。你们从民间收藏的稀缺
瑰宝在文物鉴定中严格把关，去伪存真，
我深为感叹佩，特祝贺此本立的出版展
示了祖国文化。

张如兰 2011.3.28

张如兰

北京市文物局副研究员
北京市文物鉴定委员会副主任

贺中古陶收藏
晚清官窑瓷器出版

藏珍储宝
广结古缘

辛卯 陈润民

陈润民

故宫博物院副研究员
中国古陶瓷学会理事

目 录
CONTENTS

序

　　中古陶国际艺术品公司是北京市工商局注册、北京市文物局批准的文物艺术品经营机构。总经理张常栓含辛茹苦数余载，约聘有故宫博物院、首都博物馆、国家文物鉴定委员会、文化部艺术品评估委员会等数十位专家，为国内外文物艺术品收藏爱好人士服务；同时创建了二万余件各类文物的科技鉴定数据库，从德美日古国引进了超大样品室荧光谱仪、X射线衍射仪、拉曼光谱仪等先进科技鉴定仪器，对瓷器、青铜器、漆器、玉石、珐琅、玻璃古器皿进行准确结构分析和成份分析；采用专家眼学鉴定与现代科技鉴定相结合的双轨制，对文物艺术品做出较为准确的鉴定和评估，提供诚信的交易保障。现在以日积月累收藏的珐琅瓷器集书付梓，这又是一大善举，必将利于民间收藏文物事业的进一步发展和提高。

吕济民
辛卯夏

前言 Preface

杨静荣

　　改革开放以来，随着我国整体经济水平的发展，盛世收藏的浪潮开始席卷中国大地，全国人大最新颁布的《文物法》将"藏宝于民"定为国策，中国历史上前所未有的一次收藏热潮，已经成为不可阻挡的洪流。伴随滔滔滚滚的洪流巨浪，映入人们眼帘的是一系列令人目不暇接的新生事物：私人博物馆、收藏会所、鉴定公司、画廊等等。这些崭新的机构，或创业求新，或墨守陈规；或上下求索，或滥竽充数；或求真务实，或急功近利；或默默无闻，或虚张声势；或兢兢业业，或昙花一现。可谓五花八门，鱼龙混杂，泥沙俱下。大浪淘沙之后，是金子终会闪出耀眼的光芒。中古陶就是在盛世收藏的浪潮中诞生的一个民营机构，自成立之初，便以独特的经营理念受到收藏爱好者的青睐，他们在鉴定藏品时以科技鉴定和传统鉴定相结合为手段，以求真务实为宗旨。创业十年，上下求索，终成气候，不但为广大收藏爱好者鉴定了数万件藏品，而且收藏了一批十分精彩的文物，有些甚至达到博物馆国家一级文物的标准。此次挑选部分清代晚期官窑瓷器结书出版，虽然不敢与故宫藏品媲美，但却独具风格，自成体系，另有风骚，可谓是桃李不言，遗韵成辉。

　　清代嘉庆以后开始步入晚清历史，以往学术界在评论这段中国陶瓷史时，多以"走向衰败"一言以蔽之。但是官窑烧造历史长达数百年之久，虽是步入晚期，仍然可以感觉烈士暮年、涛声依旧、晚霞遗韵、雄风犹存的壮丽辉煌。从中古陶收藏的这批藏品中也可看出端倪，其主要特征有三个：

　　一　技艺传承，经典永存

　　官窑产品精工细作，许多品种成为传统经典，历代官窑均有生产，如高温铜红釉品种，自明初发明，永乐、宣德盛行一时，以祭红称雄，到康熙时期又继承发展，除祭红外，又新创烧豇豆红和郎窑红品种。再如茶叶末釉，自雍正唐英发明后，一直延续到光绪官窑，均有生产。中古陶藏品中有嘉庆和道光五彩十二月花卉纹杯各一件，这个品种是康熙官窑开始生产的，十二个为一套，杯上绘各种不同的花纹，象征十二个月的不同季节。其完整成套者，主要收藏于北京故宫博物院。十二月花卉纹杯是宫中的实用器皿，造型工整，构思奇巧，彩绘娴熟，颇受皇帝青睐，但在使用中难免破损，所以康熙以后历代官窑继续生产，一直延续到光绪时期。中古陶收藏的这两件十二月花卉纹杯，造型和彩绘与康熙产品一脉相承，难分伯仲，如果没有款识，很难与康熙真品区别。中古陶另有两件藏品，是一对清道光窑变釉石榴尊，也是继承传统的佳作。窑变釉是唐英任督陶官时，在雍正七年（1729年），借用古代钧窑的烧成原理，使用景德镇原料发明的。窑变本是陶瓷烧成时难以控制的自然变化，唐英则纯熟地掌握其烧成工艺原理，将呈色控制在一定范围内，虽百件没有一件相同者，但是大体效果相同，给人以火爆热烈、变化万千之美感。自雍正七年（1729年）后，窑变釉在历代官窑中都有生产，且各具千秋。中古陶的这对窑变釉石榴尊，造型借用石榴果实形状，采取夸张变形写意而成，线条变化自然流畅，模拟石榴瓣的沟回处与凸起的腹面，釉色形成浓淡深浅的层次对比，使富于变化的窑变釉更增加了活泼跳跃的旋律之感，与雍正、乾隆时期同类品种比较，更显工艺纯熟。而中古陶另一件光绪火焰红釉弦纹尊，也是窑变釉的一种，与祭红釉类似，但是颜色更趋火爆，祭红釉釉层薄，至底足处不会流淌，而窑变釉釉层厚，至底足处多有流淌，这是区分二者的鉴定要领。此件火焰红釉弦纹尊呈色浓艳，不比雍正、乾隆产品逊色，但是书写了光绪官款，总让人联想到夕阳晚霞的余晖。珐琅彩、洋彩和粉彩是近几年收藏界乐于争论的课题，起因是台北故宫博物院《华丽彩瓷》一书的出版，台北故宫学者根据清宫档案记载，正本清源，指出"粉彩"一词是郭葆昌先生在上个世纪三十年代最早提出使用的，清宫旧藏的一批乾隆六年至九年（1741-1744年）烧造的过去定名珐琅彩或粉彩的彩瓷，在原档案中命名"洋彩"，这批瓷器是在景德镇御窑厂烧造的，主要藏于台北故宫博物院，达500件之多，北京故宫博物院也有部分收藏，台北故宫博物院于2008年举办特展，展示出这批瓷器的一部分，并且出版了《华丽彩瓷》。类似的瓷器在北京故宫虽然没有数百件，但是也有一定数量的收藏，如乾隆万年甲子历转颈笔筒，北京故宫收藏的那件为蓝地（台北故宫为黄地），再如米黄釉瓶、胭脂红地瓶、茶叶末描金瓶等等，均与台北故宫收藏的是同一个时期生产的瓷器。我在北京故宫整理这批瓷器时，感到最棘手的是特别容易与珐琅彩混淆，在文物登记卡片上，老专家也在二者之间变化。之所以会出现这种情况，主要是因为所谓的"洋彩"中，有一部分彩料与珐琅彩相同。清宫档案中记载的乾隆六年至九年（1741-1744年）洋彩瓷器是在景德镇烧成的，而珐琅彩瓷器主要是在宫中造办处烧造。在郭葆昌提出粉彩一词之前，只有珐琅彩和洋彩之称，因为"粉彩"更加通俗易懂，遂在学术界开始流行至今。清宫档案和文献记载的许多名称与现在用词不同，在陶瓷史中常见，如茶叶末釉，本是唐英发明，他在文献中明确记载叫"厂官釉"，但是古玩界却一直叫茶叶末釉，因为通俗易通，故沿用，只有非常专业的研究者才了解其来龙去脉，但想纠正习惯势力，恐不是一朝一夕可以完成的。其实在景德镇的老艺人中，一直都把粉彩叫洋彩，直到解放后还是如此称之。《华丽彩瓷》出版后，最兴奋的是收藏界，都争先恐后把手中收藏的粉彩瓷器更名为洋彩。笔者认为其实大可不必，藏品的水平高低，不是在于名称，还是得看实物。中古陶收藏清道光粉彩轧道黄地圆光四季山水人物膳碗一对，黄地颜料从感观观察，应该是使用的珐琅彩料中锑黄颜料，虽然能否定名为洋彩尚可研讨，但是其工整的造型、规整的图案、娴熟的画风，确实可以和乾隆洋彩媲美。此外，中古陶收藏的清道光青花龙纹盘、清道光冬青刻暗团花纹碗、清道光珊瑚红地描金彩绘缠枝宝相花纹碗、清道光斗彩碗、斗彩杯以及清光绪青花赏瓶、清光绪祭蓝釉象耳琮式瓶等器物，均是继承康熙、雍正、乾隆时期传统的成熟作品，可谓是一脉相承，不让须眉。

二 传世珍稀，收藏热点

清代晚期历史多乱，官窑烧造曾经一度中断，传世品稀少，遂成为收藏家收藏的热点。咸丰四年（1854年），太平军攻占景德镇，出于朴素的阶级感情，一把大火烧了御窑厂，并且在景德镇留下一个烧太平窑的民俗。如何评价太平军的功过，是历史学家的任务；如何看待烧太平窑的民俗，是社会学家的事情。咸丰皇帝多难，御窑厂烧了，英法联军又把圆明园烧了，官窑瓷器损失严重，以致至今北京和台北故宫收藏的咸丰官窑瓷器十分稀少。物以稀为贵，在收藏界能收到咸丰官窑瓷器均被视为莫大的幸事。中古陶收藏一件清咸丰黄地轧道粉彩开光三羊开泰纹大碗，造型端庄，彩绘工整，图案吉祥，是颇为难得的咸丰粉彩瓷器的经典之作。到同治时期，太平天国运动失败，东西宫治理朝政，御窑厂重新开工，许多身怀绝技的陶工尚未全部召回，虽然开工了，仍然生产官窑瓷器，但是却显露出恢复期的稚拙之感。中古陶收藏同治天蓝釉罐一件，底青花竖书双行楷书"大清同治年制"款。天蓝釉在康熙、雍正、乾隆时期的官窑，是一个十分名贵的品种，北京和台北的故宫博物院藏品中数量不多，同治官窑更是传世稀少。中古陶的这件藏品，虽不能与康乾盛世时期的官窑同类作品媲美，但小巧精致，釉色纯正，可以看出官窑作品不惜工本、精工细作的优良传统，作为收藏家的把玩之物，颇具收藏价值。中古陶收藏一件宣统蓝釉壶，底竖书双行青花楷书"大清宣统年制"款，仔细观察，壶的肩部印有暗花，暗花凸起处有出筋露白现象，整体蓝釉形成浓淡深浅的层次变化，使单一纯正的釉色增加了韵律的美感。宣统只有三年，官窑传世品更为稀少，能收藏一件宣统官窑瓷器，其中的乐趣，只有收藏者本人能够说清。中古陶还收藏了几件民国早期瓷器，均为彩瓷。民国彩瓷现在均以珠山八友为热点，其实还有两点应该值得收藏家重视。一个是民国早期那些曾经在御窑厂工作过的能工巧匠仍然在世，他们生产的仿古瓷器几可与官窑媲美。中古陶收藏的光绪款粉彩描金开光如意吉祥小渣斗一对，应该就是民国早期的这种高仿官窑瓷器。另一个是与郭葆昌有关的彩瓷，郭葆昌自称的"洪宪"瓷器，至今仍是历史谜案，但是从郭葆昌捐献给故宫的瓷器观察（其实物现存北京故宫博物院），应该是郭葆昌在景德镇请彩绘高手定制的瓷器，底款多书"觯斋主人"，其画工精细工整，注重技法和技艺，与珠山八友注重意境和理念的文人风格有别。中古陶收藏的民国粉彩耄耋纹瓶、粉彩绘折枝玉兰翠竹题诗马蹄杯及粉彩虞美人图题诗瓶一对均属于和郭葆昌先生捐献给故宫的彩瓷同一类的作品，粉彩绘折枝玉兰翠竹题诗马蹄杯及粉彩虞美人图题诗瓶一对的彩料中可能有洋彩成分，收藏家更愿意说成"珐琅彩"。中古陶的藏品中，最具收藏价值的，应该是光绪描金矾红彩云龙纹登，这种登是皇宫用的祭器，容易和豆混淆，传世品中豆较为常见，登十分稀少，其造型端庄大方，线条转折变换流畅，画工极为工整，洁白的胎釉在金彩和矾红彩映衬下，给人以庄严肃穆的皇家至尊之感。如果不仔细观察龙纹的细微特征，几可看成乾隆鼎盛之作，器物周身所绘九条龙，虽然姿态各异，神猛依旧，但是画风眼神则显现出光绪时期桑榆晚霞的时代特征，正映照了本书帝国余晖的命名。

三 传统科技，双管齐下

本书藏品，即使那些来源于著名拍卖行的藏品，也是既经过专家传统眼学的鉴定，又经过科技检测的验证，双管齐下，保证失误率降到最低点，实属可贵。中古陶一直遵循双轨制鉴定原则，传统鉴定由北京故宫博物院、国家博物馆、首都博物馆、景德镇陶瓷学院的部分专家、教授以及部分在实践中取得了成功经验的人员进行。科技检测则购置了最先进的进口设备，而且科技检测的实际操作均由中国科学院和中国矿产资源研究所的专家指导进行，在检测瓷器新老的技术方面，遥遥领先。令我佩服的是曾经有一件老底冷接瓶身的器物，传统鉴定根本看不出冷接的天衣无缝的接痕，在科技检测时，则准确的给出了底足是元代的、瓶身是现代的结论；还有一件器物，明代早期的底足，冷接了一个清代的瓶身，在检测中，也未逃脱科学仪器的客观结论。

虽然中古陶在业内已经开创了自己的品牌，而且得到众多收藏爱好者的认可，但是他们一直低调行事，可谓是桃李不言下自成蹊。据我所知，中古陶还收藏了不少成系列的精彩藏品，希望能早日成书，与广大收藏爱好者共同交流。

收藏赋 Collection Fu

路东之

宇宙时空，何谓始终；地球经纬，交织纵横。人类文明，延绵亘古；收藏文化，一脉传承。华夏我土，物华天宝；炎黄子孙，人杰地灵。

或问，何谓收藏？呜呼！一语难定。究其行止，察其性质，无非求物以聚，集器以宝；珍之、爱之、赏之、品之、语之、问之、识之、论之；盖为我有，乃为我用，聊通我心，以寄我志。

或问：收藏何者？宇内之物，无不可藏；尘间万类，无不堪宝；陶玉金银，咸成美器，木骨皮壳，俱博美名。

或问：藏者何为？人之有欲，其欲足贪；人之有瘾，其瘾足大；人之有念，其念悠悠；人之有想，佳想安善。

或问：收藏何益？或曰积少成多，或曰聚财成富；或曰陶冶性情，或曰怡养心智；或曰寄傲托怀，或曰修身励志；或曰考古发微，或曰补遗正史；或曰教化民众，或曰启迪后生；或曰弘扬传统，或曰传承文明。

或问：收藏何患？或曰痴心妄想，或曰贪心不足；或曰斗富使气，或曰妒嫉比攀；或曰狭胸小器，或曰患得患失；或曰明珠投暗，或曰密不示人；或曰完残太计，或曰唯利是图；或曰盲从趋众，或曰真伪无明。

呜呼！其为收藏，源之人性；老壑深渊，地久天长。

然则，人之有私，其私唯我；人之有触，其触为敌。

长安有刘汉基叟，暮年尝其子曰："吾人收藏，其所玩者何也？盖玩其我有你没有哉！" 一时传为前辈收藏家之遗训真言。

然则，人之善群，结觉营邦；人之善友，莫逆成赏；人之有朋，近方远方；人之有善，与人分享。

然则，人之亦藏，我之亦藏；人之或有，我或无有；我之所爱，人亦所爱；我之所爱，人或非爱；人或所多，我或所少；人或所轻，我或所重；我或所失，人或所拾；人或所弃，我或所取。

此大千世界滚滚红尘，熙熙攘攘人间世象，皆事故人情也。亦每使世人忧愁烦恼，爱恨疑迷，徒添悲悔苦痛哉！

然则，或问藏于何处为宜？答曰可以各得其所。以天子之尊无能独占尽得，以邦国之大岂堪全保通收；以皓首之苍犹见执著意态，以黄童之稚亦显迷戏情怀；以个命之微屡构规模体系，以万民之力足可众志成城。嗟乎！倘世人都怀良知，各有觉悟；咸出本力，各得其所；俱出公心，皆呈爱意，咸以真诚，各尽美奥；则人人分乐人人，处处共享处处；则天下之宝人类共有，"天下为公"人间可期；则人类遗产得保得弘，人类文明得传得炽。盖本当既"藏宝于国"亦"藏宝于民"也，而"藏宝于民"犹"藏宝于国"矣！

然则，君子者流，何行何所？藏界众生，何去何从？邦国之法，如何修正？世界之规，怎样达成？

此吾侪同心协力，天下先忧者也。

追想当初，廿二载前，路子负笈长安之初，浅知收藏，痴心觅宝，偶感灵机，略显癫相。尝于西北大学图书馆工地妙得"菩萨残碑"，读出"有菩萨不住色""六字神谕"际，忽觉灵腑洞穿，魂开一窍。从此倾情收藏，痴心不坠。尝于随后所作《菩萨残碑记——梦斋收藏笔记之一》中言："东之以为君子者所谓收藏，本藏与自己而非昭之他人。故其所藏之物也，当不重于世之行情何如，他人眼中怎样。实在缘之深浅，情之薄厚，通灵几何！盖天下万般，两者之间唯缘是载。为缘而聚，乏缘则疏，无缘而不相逢也。世之人也贪慕珍宝，而所谓世之珍宝者又能几多又谁尽得之？而况尘间万类以彼观之皆虚诞也。若为心和缘汇而神通，虽一石一木皆宝皆珍。反之，虽珍宝美玉又土石何异哉！古今达贵者流，每以千金易得一物而不能识，昭之隐之俱枉然也！何若我一块顽石，两行残字，乐此奇缘也！"

呜呼，此少时语耳，少时境矣！然梦斋收藏考古之旅由兹发轫，痴心无悔，奇缘不绝，竟成壮举。并于公元一九九六年秋，成立中国首批私立博物馆之古陶文明博物馆。屈指回眸，开馆亦十三载矣！光阴如梭而天地恒亘，白云飘渺而日月长辉；梦斋多徙而陶馆难移，书生老去而壮志犹存。

中古陶（北京）国际艺术品有限公司坐落于故都南池子大街七号。楼阁虽小，犹矗四层，乃历百年之古建筑。民国初年内务总长朱启钤规划故都际，由法兰西工程师设计修造，其风格样式合璧中西。"中古陶人"于此构筑鉴定、展览、交流、典当、服务平台。崇檀女史殷勤索赋，引领观瞻，命题作文。有所谓"是赋非路子为之不可"语。

路子既来，诗则在腑。乃登斯楼，但见布局蕴巧，依稀坛府之属；陈列精当，弥然雅所之境。展卷垂幅，浏览书墙画壁；布玉陈瓷，品察沁色窑温。

及至顶层，推窗而望，妙景忽开。平瞻紫禁，黄瓦排金烁彩；送目煤山，高亭次第情真。草木临轩，秋虫偶自鸣唱；花果坠地，燕雀忽尔离群；宅第长街，四时风雨顺顺，皇城永巷，朝暮雾霭纷纷；投眸北海，琼岛云霞铺彩；远眺西山，庙宇气韵氤氲。

得此妙处，朋交知音之属，香茗慢饮；美食贪酒之辈，佳酿倾樽；鸿儒雅量之士，以藏会友；谦谦好学之侣，精进知新；把玩美器，时常赏鉴故物；探问交流，偶尔俯仰古今。岂不悠哉妙哉！

◈ 路东之

古陶文明博物馆馆长。

1　清光绪　矾红描金蟠龙纹豆

高29厘米　口径16.5厘米　足径16.5厘米

Deng decorated with iron-red design of coiled dragons
Guangxu period, Qing Dynasty
Height: 29cm, Diameter of mouth: 16.5cm, Diameter
of foot: 16.5cm

　　高柄，圈足，顶端为子母口盖盒状，盖圆，宝珠形钮，造型庄重沉稳，胎质洁白细腻，釉色匀净鲜亮，通体以矾红彩描金绘形态各异的九条龙，画面层次分明，繁而不乱，矾红彩呈色纯正，画法娴熟。其所绘九龙身形瘦劲，平滑无鳞，背部龙鳍参差。挺胸，头回首，神态威猛张扬。"大清光绪年制"刻款。为光绪官窑上乘之作，在已经发表的文献著录中，未见相同的器物，可能为孤品。

　　祭祀崇拜宇宙天地和神灵先祖，是千百年来每一个封建王朝皇帝的头等大事，而祭祀所用的仪式程序与器具，更是章典规范，一丝不苟。根据乾隆三十年编修的《皇朝礼器图式》中所记载，簦于乾隆十三年被正式钦定为祭器之一，用于天坛、祈谷坛、地坛、朝日坛、夕月坛、太岁坛、太庙正殿、文庙的祭祀，其级别之高及重要性可见一斑。其中，《图式》卷二祭器二的图绘所见的太庙正殿的装饰为蟠龙纹，与本件矾红描金簦完全相同。簦是官窑瓷祭器中相对少见的品类，也经常与豆混淆，其区别在于簦的盖子上是宝珠钮，而豆的盖子上则是绞绳钮。

⊙ 参考文献

清允禄等编撰、牧东点校《皇朝礼器图式》，广陵书社，2004年，第41页。

Horse-hoof-shaped bowl with posy design in contrasting colors
Daoguang period, Qing Dynasty
Height: 6.6cm, Diameter of mouth: 15.2cm, Diameter of foot: 9cm

　　碗广口、斜直壁、圈足。足底青花篆书六字
三行"大清道光年制"款，其造型类似倒置的马
蹄，故俗称"马蹄式碗"。成化斗彩世所称著，清
代官窑视其为楷模，多有仿制，但色彩比成化更加
丰富。该碗外壁主题纹饰绘四个团型花果，团花间
环饰石榴纹。构图简洁疏朗，画工娴熟。类似的品
种，乾隆、嘉庆、道光官窑均有烧制。做工精美程
度，难分伯仲。

⊙ 参考文献

东莞市博物馆编《东莞市博物馆藏陶瓷》，文物出版社·2010年·第70页图63。

3 清道光　青花云龙纹大盘
高5厘米　口径25厘米　足径16.5厘米
Blue and white plate with cloud-and-dragon design
Daoguang period, Qing Dynasty
Height: 5cm, Diameter of mouth: 25cm, Diameter of foot: 16.5cm

　　青花龙纹盘为明清官窑的传统品种，历代官窑
均有生产。该盘盘心绘云龙纹，龙纹周围火焰密布，
动感强烈。盘外壁绘双龙赶珠纹，画法工整。盘底青
花书"大清道光年制"六字三行篆书款。

碗深弧腹，撇口，圈足，该造型明代中期定型，俗称〝宫碗〞，也称〝正德碗〞，其造型舒展大方，使用方便。碗心彩绘描金宝相花，外壁以明亮柔和的浅黄釉为地，锥剔出流畅工整的凤尾卷草花纹，四个圆形开光内分别以粉彩、墨彩绘出《踏雪寻梅》、《携琴访友》、《秋山访寺》、《寒江独钓》故事纹，是表现文人雅趣的传统图案。四个开光间绘格式化的折枝西莲花，底足内青花横书篆体双行〝大清道光年制〞款。

这种在色地上轧道再绘开光景物花卉的宫碗，寓意锦上添花，是乾隆六年至八年开始烧造的名贵官窑品种，内务府造办处的《活计档》中有记载说明这种色地轧道开光碗是当时奉旨定烧之物，曾于乾隆至道光年间流行一时，有天蓝地、胭脂地、粉色地、浅黄地、深蓝地等品种，开光内容也分博古、山水、花卉、三羊及人物等，以制作精良、手法繁复、绘制精美而著称，体现出不惜工本追求完美的官窑品质。磁胎洋彩圆光膳碗，在乾隆烧造始，即受到朝廷格外重视，烧造数量稀少，皆装上好匣囊，成对存放于紫禁城中最重要的宫殿——乾清宫，可见其地位非同一般。道光皇帝以节俭治国而著称，故官窑瓷器多遵循前朝岁例贡瓷，量少而精，时有逸品，予人清新脱俗之感，其细腻之作亦为藏家所爱。其中雍乾之际的御瓷名品也深受道光皇帝所喜爱，遂命临摹烧造，得原作之精髓，画意之清雅逸致毫不逊色，颇得乾隆古韵。相似的轧道碗在国内外著名博物馆也有收藏，如美国旧金山亚洲艺术博物馆藏一件相同作品，而成对的传世品，完美无瑕者，则是难得一见。

⊙ **参考文献**

He Li, Chinese Ceramics—The New Standard Guide from the Asian Art Museum of San Francisco, Thames & Hudson, London, 2006, page 308, plate 669.

香港艺术馆《清朝瑰宝》，南天书局，1992年，第323页图190。

叶佩兰主编《故宫博物院藏文物珍品大系——珐琅彩·粉彩》，上海科学技术出版社、香港商务印书馆，1999年，第119页。

香港苏富比拍卖，2005年11月28日，第1353号。

5

清光绪　青花缠枝莲花纹赏瓶

高38.6厘米　口径9.9厘米　足径13厘米

Blue and white vase with interlocking lotus sprays
Guangxu period, Qing Dynasty
Height: 38.6cm, Diameter of mouth: 9.9cm,
Diameter of foot: 13cm

大清光
緒年製

　　瓶撇口，长颈，肩凸起弦纹，圆腹，圈足。通体以青花为饰，口部绘海水波浪纹，其下绘如意纹一周，颈部绘蕉叶纹和回纹，肩部绘缠枝花卉，并有如意纹与口部对应。腹部主体为缠枝莲，其下绘莲瓣纹，圈足外壁绘卷草纹。底青花竖书双行"大清光绪年制"六字楷书款。

　　赏瓶因多用于皇帝赏赐下臣而得名，纹饰多为青花缠枝莲纹，取其"青"、"莲"谐音，寓意"清廉"，希望臣下为官清正廉明。自雍正开始，历代官窑均有生产。该瓶造型工整，画工娴熟，是一件标准的官窑器。

⊙ 参考文献

耿宝昌主编《故宫博物院藏文物珍品大系—青花釉里红（下）》，上海科学技术出版社，香港商务印书馆，2000年，第174页，第159号。

清道光　斗彩缠枝花卉纹碗（一对）

高7厘米　口径14厘米　足径5.3厘米

A pair of bowls with design of interlocking lotus in contrasting colors
Daoguang period, Qing Dynasty
Height: 7cm, Diameter of mouth: 14cm, Diameter of foot: 5.3cm

碗撇口，弧腹，圈足。胎体轻巧、色白，质细密。碗外壁以斗彩绘缠枝花卉纹，画法细腻工整。外底心以青料书写"大清道光年制"六字三行青花篆书款，字体工整，笔画苍劲有力。是道光御窑仿制雍正朝的仿古作品，其造型、胎釉、画工，均可与雍正真品媲美，堪称拟古佳作。

⊙ 参考文献

故宫博物院编、耿宝昌主编

《孙瀛洲的陶瓷世界》，紫禁城出

版社，2005年，第218页图133。

清道光 珊瑚红地金彩缠枝宝相花纹碗

高5.4厘米 口径11.8厘米 足径4.3厘米

Bowl with design of flowers in gold enamels on coral-red ground
Daoguang period, Qing Dynasty
Height: 5.4cm, Diameter of mouth: 11.8cm, Diameter of foot: 4.3cm

　　碗弧壁，敞腹，直口，圈足，造型端庄典雅，为典型的宫廷膳用器皿。外壁以珊瑚红为地，以金彩绘缠枝宝相花和五福拱寿纹。足内白釉书青花篆书"大清道光年制"款。胎骨轻盈薄透，坚致雪白，敷彩华丽浓重，吉祥喜庆，具有强烈的宫廷艺术装饰风格。

　　以氧化铁为呈色剂的珊瑚红与金彩，都属于低温釉彩，红金二色对比热烈而喜庆，装饰效果华丽，故一直是宫廷器物上比较常见的装饰手法，但此二色乃低温彩炉中烘烤而成，在使用中容易磨损剥落，保存不易，故传世珊瑚红金彩器物多伤彩严重，完整无损者难得一见。

　　北京故宫博物院珍藏了几件道光珊瑚红地金彩瓷，如一件盖罐与一把勺，另北京华辰拍卖公司也曾拍卖过一对海棠式小花盆，这些瓷器均落"慎德堂制"款，皆作珊瑚红地金彩宝相花纹与五福拱寿纹，与这件碗的纹样完全相同。"慎德堂"是道光皇帝在圆明园中的一处起居室名称，故"慎德堂"款的瓷器就是道光皇帝御用之物。这件碗书六字年号款，造型与纹饰与"慎德堂"款器完全一样，珊瑚红彩与金彩的色相也一模一样，故也应是道光官窑膳食用器皿。

⊙ **参考文献**

耿宝昌、吕成龙主编《故宫博物院藏文物珍品大系—杂釉彩·素三彩》，2009年，第213、214、216页，图171~174。

民国　仿珐琅彩题诗耄耋图小瓶

高10.5厘米　口径4.1厘米　足径3.8厘米

Vase decorated with cat and butterfly design in cloisonne enamel
Republic period
Height: 10.5cm, Diameter of mouth: 4.1cm, Diameter of foot: 3.8cm

雍乾之后，彩瓷成为景德镇的主流产品，到民国时期尤为盛行，尤其是仿古之作，不惜工本，佳料为之成胎，良匠为之彩画，所出之作，几可乱真。该瓶造型小巧轻盈，胎骨轻薄，宛如脱胎，是民国仿珐琅彩瓷的特点之一。其釉质光洁莹润，主题纹饰为耄耋图，是传统祝寿的吉祥图案，狸猫仰望彩蝶之神态生动逼真，饶有情趣。周边山石层叠，质感强烈，一如乾隆时期之皴法。百合花开，芳香四溢，娇黄设色，灿烂夺目。空白处题诗"花间蝶自舞，狸何叫不休。"前后钤印"仁化"、"世宁"、"碧露"三章。"乾隆年制"蓝料楷书款。构图画法均源自宫廷用瓷，属民国精品之作。

中国古代尊称八十岁以上的老人为耄耋，而"猫蝶"与"耄耋"谐音，故民间常将猫、蝶组合在一起，寓意"耄耋"，作为对人们长寿的祝福，是民间最为常见的吉祥图案之一。此瓶估计应是一件精心制作，奉呈给老年长者的祝寿礼物。

花
間
蝶

自
舞

狸
何
叫

不
休

9 民国　仿珐琅彩虞美人题诗瓶（一对）

高20.5厘米　口径4.7厘米　足径5.8厘米

A pair of vases decorated with poppy design in cloisonne enamel
Republic period
Height: 20.5cm, Diameter of mouth: 4.7cm, Diameter of foot: 5.8cm

瓶胎骨极轻薄，宛如脱胎，胎质洁白坚致。瓶颈以蓝料彩绘璎珞纹一周；圈足上也呼应以蓝料彩绘雷纹一周。瓶身一面以珐琅料彩混合粉彩绘虞美人一丛，另一面以黑彩题写五言短诗两句，诗首末匀绘胭脂料彩印章。两件瓶彩料精纯艳丽，笔法细致入微，使用诗配画的构图，是非常典型的民国仿雍乾珐琅彩瓷的特点与手法，这种精美的民国瓷器，当时被称为"古月轩"瓷，价高而难得，倍受珍视。

景德镇官窑随着中华民国的成立也宣告结束。御窑厂的能工巧匠流落民间，遂形成了景德镇民国瓷器的两个亮点，一个是以"珠山八友"为代表的彩绘瓷器，另一个就是仿古瓷器的大量生产。前者颇具文人气息，后者则以量大质精颇受收藏者青睐。郭葆昌自称在1915年至1916年间为袁世凯"登基"烧制了4万余件"洪宪御瓷"而名闻天下。此为学术界一宗谜案，实物一件无存。郭葆昌1946年曾将自己在景德镇定烧的瓷器捐献给故宫博物院，现分存于北京和台北故宫博物院。底款书"觯斋主人"，其主要品种就是这种仿珐琅彩的瓶类，绘画技法工整娴熟，与御窑厂的能工巧匠如出一辙。

近3年来，民国瓷器中的精品逐渐被收藏家和市场所认识和接受，并由于流通数量的稀缺，民国彩瓷的价格迅速攀升。最近在纽约苏富比拍出的一件民国仿乾隆粉彩橄榄瓶，创造了新的民国瓷器价格记录。

⊙ 参考文献

纽约苏富比拍卖，2011年3月22日，戴润斋专场，第119号。民国仿乾隆粉彩花卉纹橄榄瓶，成交价：131.45万美元。

北京保利拍卖，2010年6月4日春季拍卖会，第4313号。民国（1947年）珐琅彩开光山水如意代尊，高32厘米。

含芳扣

弓意

呈彩亦

當時

含芳和
弓意
呈彩亦
当时

民国 粉彩折枝玉兰翠竹纹题诗马蹄杯

高5厘米 口径8.8厘米 足径5厘米

Horse-hoof-shaped cup decorated with design of plucked
sprays of magnolia in famille rose
Republic period
Height: 5cm, Diameter of mouth: 8.8cm, Diameter of foot: 5cm

　　杯撇口，深腹，平底，圈足，体呈马蹄状。外壁饰粉彩玉
兰花，杯内底心彩绘一朵玉兰花，外底书蓝料宋体"乾隆年制"
款。胎体轻薄，画工精细，诗画一体，情景交融，具有强烈的
艺术感染力，是民国仿官窑的精品之作，可惜没有成套保存。

　　此种杯式又称十二月花卉纹杯，除粉彩外尚有五彩制成的，
始盛于康熙时期。

⊙ **参考文献**

叶佩兰主编《故宫博物院藏文物珍品大系—珐琅彩·粉彩》，上海科学技术出版社、香港商务印书馆，1999年，第236～239页图211。

二人對
酌山花
開

清道光　窑变釉花口六棱石榴尊（一对）

高19.8厘米　口径10.8厘米　足径9.4厘米

A pair of flambe-glazed pomegranate-shaped vessels
Daoguang period, Qing Dynasty
Height: 19.8cm Diameter of mouth: 10.8cm, Diameter of foot: 9.4cm

尊通体作瓜棱式造型，口沿外翻，束颈，圆鼓腹，圈足微外撇。釉面凸出部位为红色，呈现红宝石般的光泽，凹下的颈及口沿面呈天蓝色，唇边一线为月白色，给人以变化万千之感。底足有阴文"大清道光年制"篆书印章款。

窑变釉是唐英于雍正七年（1729年）后新发明的釉色品种，同样的器物在乾隆官窑器中多见，而于道光官窑器中比较少见。

⊙ 参考文献

《中国陶瓷全集》第15卷 清
（下）·上海人民美术出版社·
2000年·第178页图169。

碗撇口，深弧腹，圈足。胎质细腻，通体施白釉，釉面莹润。外壁以粉彩为饰，以粉、黄、绿、墨诸色绘花鸟纹，花枝婆娑蔓延，环绕碗腹一周，飞鸟翱翔其间，给人以鸟语花香、生机盎然之感。碗底书"大清光绪年制"六字双行楷书款，是典型的光绪官窑器。

⊙ 参考文献

叶佩兰主编《故宫博物院藏文物珍品大系——珐琅彩·粉彩》，上海科学技术出版社、香港商务印书馆，1999年，第118页图102。

13 清同治　白釉绿彩云龙纹盘

高4.5厘米　口径18.3厘米　足径11.3厘米

Plate decorated with green design of dragon
and cloud over a white ground
Tongzhi period, Qing Dynasty
Height: 4.5cm, Diameter of mouth: 18.3cm,
Diameter of foot: 11.3cm

盘撇口，浅弧壁，圈足。盘内底及外壁均在白色釉地上装饰绿彩云龙纹。其做法是：先在成型后的坯体上锥拱云龙纹，然后将花纹以外的地子施以透明釉，入窑经高温烧成后，再在露胎的花纹处填涂绿彩，并在釉上描绘龙的须、爪、肘、毛等细部，复入窑经低温彩烧而成，外底书青花楷书"大清同治年制"六字双行款。

白釉绿彩瓷器最早见于明代成化时景德镇御器厂制品，造型有盘、碗等。弘治、正德、嘉靖时均沿袭烧造。清代并不多见，同治时期能烧造这样的品种实属难得，此品种传世品比较稀少。

大清同
治年製

大清同
治年製

◎ 参考文献

故宫博物院编、耿宝昌主编《孙瀛洲的陶瓷世界》，紫禁城出版社，2005年，第110页。

耿宝昌、吕成龙主编《故宫博物院藏文物珍品大系—杂釉彩·素三彩》，上海科学技术出版社，香港商务印书馆，2009年，第96页图77。

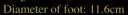

14 清光绪　霁蓝釉象耳琮式瓶

高30厘米　口径9.3厘米　足径11.6厘米

Cong-shaped vase with two elephant-
shaped ears in sky-clearing blue glaze
Guangxu period, Qing Dynasty
Height: 30cm, Diameter of mouth: 9.3cm,
Diameter of foot: 11.6cm

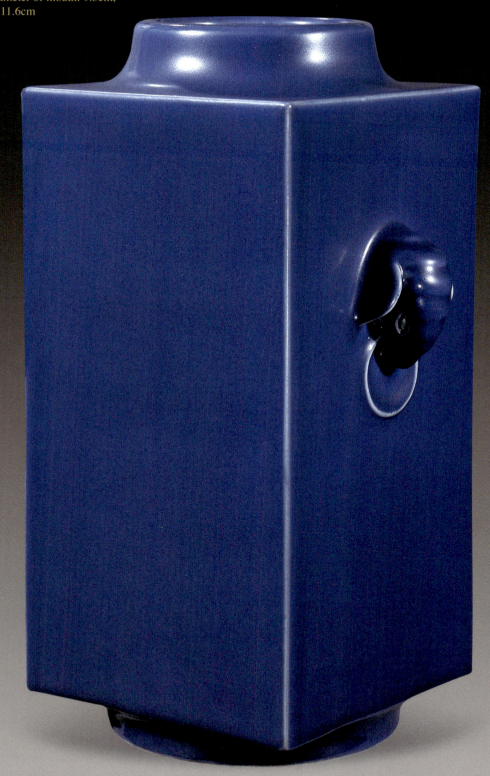

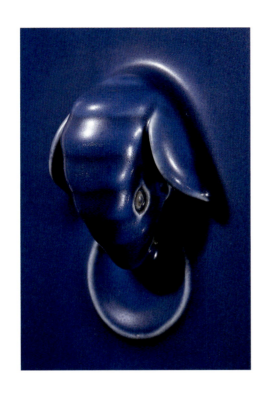

瓶直口，短颈，平肩，方腹，平底，圈足。腹上部对称置象头铺首，象鼻衔环。通体内外及外底均施霁蓝釉，釉色均匀、亮丽。瓶口、棱角及象耳、鼻、环等转折凸起处均隐显白色胎骨。外底霁蓝釉下青花书"大清光绪年制"六字双行楷书款。

蓝釉的呈色剂为氧化钴，高温钴蓝釉瓷器出现于元代，传世品不多。明代早期的铜红釉、祭蓝釉和甜白釉瓷器，曾被后人评为三大上品。清代霁蓝釉瓷器历朝均有精品传世，常见造型仍是祭器和陈设器，所以霁蓝也叫"祭蓝"。琮是方器，景德镇称为"镶器"，制作时难度较大，烧成的成品率也较低。该琮式瓶釉色纯正、造型端庄，反映出清代晚期官窑仍然一丝不苟、不计工本、工艺纯熟的真实面貌。

⊙ 参考文献

故宫博物院编、耿宝昌主编《孙瀛洲的陶瓷世界》，紫禁城出版社，2005年，第268页图166。

15 清同治　天蓝釉小罐

高7.7厘米 口径3.7厘米 足径 3.8 厘米

Jar in sky-blue glaze
Tongzhi period, Qing Dynasty
Height: 7.7cm, Diameter of mouth: 3.7cm,
Diameter of foot: 3.8cm

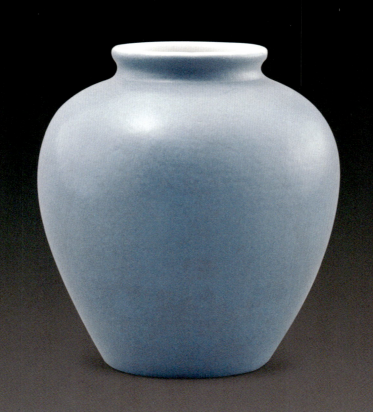

　　罐唇口、丰肩，肩以下渐收敛，圈足，底竖书青花六字双行楷书"大清同治年制"款。整体造型端庄小巧，线条转换流畅自然。外壁施天蓝釉，罐内及底足施白釉，做工极为工整。咸丰官窑毁于战火，到同治时期重新开窑，许多品种都在恢复和重新创制之中。天蓝釉在明初即已烧造，康雍乾时达到高峰。天蓝釉是十分名贵的品种，霁蓝、回青等高温釉的钴含量均在2%左右，如果降低其钴含量到1%以下，则可烧成天蓝色高温釉。但是即使在北京和台北的故宫博物院中，这个品种存世量也比较少。此罐继承前朝传统，釉色纯正，凝聚着同治官窑的沧桑历史，而且同治天蓝釉传世品比较罕见，更显其珍贵的收藏价值。

大清同
治年製

⊙ 参考文献

杨静荣主编《故宫博物院藏文
物珍品大系——颜色釉》，上海科
学技术出版社、香港商务印书馆，
1999年，第94～97页图87～89。

16 清光绪　黄釉刻云龙纹盘（一对）

高3.9厘米　口径17.5厘米　足径11厘米

A pair of yellow glazed plates with veiled
decoration of dragon among clouds
Guangxu period, Qing Dynasty
Height: 3.9cm, Diameter of mouth: 17.5cm,
Diameter of foot: 11cm

盘敞口，弧壁，圈足，底微塌。此盘造型呈窝状，故俗称"窝盘"。通体施黄釉，盘心暗刻一条矫健的行龙，外壁也暗刻行龙。底足内施白釉，书青花"大清光绪年制"六字双行楷书款。

低温黄釉瓷创烧于明初景德镇官窑，"黄"与"皇"谐音，黄色是皇家尊贵的象征，民窑不许烧造，据乾隆时期文献记载，即使烧坏的残次品也全部送到京城销毁，防止技术外流，由此可知黄釉瓷器在皇宫中被珍视的程度。该盘是典型的御窑厂黄釉瓷器。

大清光
绪年製

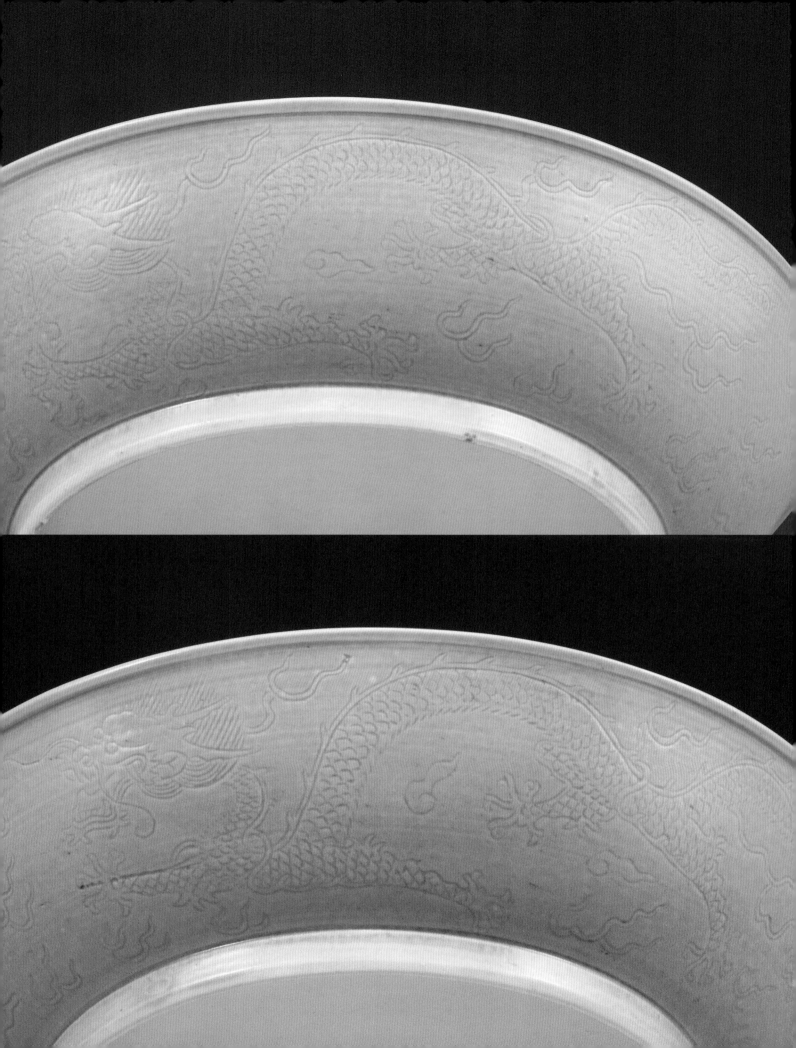

⊙ **参考文献**

杨静荣主编《故宫博物院藏文

物珍品大系——颜色釉》，上海科

学技术出版社，香港商务印书馆，

1999年，第39页图35、第44页图

39。

　　碗口微外敞，深弧腹，圈足。足脊露胎，胎骨坚致，胎体轻巧，造型规整，制作精细。通体施东青釉，釉色纯正。外壁暗刻团莲瓣纹饰，外底面施青白釉，底心落"大清道光年制"六字三行青花篆书款。

　　东青釉亦称"冻青釉"、"冬青釉"，据说北宋东窑瓷釉呈淡青色，故名。明景德镇有专仿东青户。青釉是以铁为着色剂在还原焰中烧制而成的，其含铁量一般均在3％以下。这种传统的高温釉是中国陶瓷史上最早出现的釉，且青釉瓷器一直是中国瓷器的主要产品，历经了东汉、六朝、唐、宋、元至明、清不绝。明清景德镇窑继承龙泉青瓷的优良传统，烧出了深浅不同的各种青釉瓷器，但直到清雍正时才达到了呈色均匀、稳定的烧造水平。青釉呈色深浅不同，一般仅是从色泽上划分类别：淡青色称粉青，稍深者为东青，最深者称豆青。其中东青釉尤为珍贵。

⊙ **参考文献**

杨静荣主编《故宫博物院藏文物珍品大系—颜色釉》，上海科学技术出版社、香港商务印书馆，1999年，第136页图124、第139页图127。

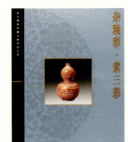

清光绪　窑变釉弦纹筝齐尊

高13厘米　口径5.8厘米　足径8厘米

Flambe glazed water-chestnuts-shaped
vase with bow string pattern
Guangxu period, Qing Dynasty
Height: 13cm, Diameter of mouth: 5.8cm,
Diameter of foot: 8cm

　　该尊造型仿荸荠而成，故俗称荸荠尊，也称荸荠瓶。其线条转折变化简练大方，仅在扁腹上起一道弦纹，通体施肥厚凝重的窑变釉，深沉的红色与局部华丽的紫蓝色交融，带来视觉上丰富的流动感，圈足内施酱釉，竖刻双行六字楷书"大清光绪年制"款。

　　窑变釉是单色釉瓷器中最变幻无穷、引人入胜的作品。它呈色的机制，是因为釉料中含有多种不同的金属氧化物，在窑烧过程中，因为氧化或还原的窑室气氛变化而自然产生出来的釉色。这些釉色随机自然地流淌交融在一起，形成了红、白、蓝、紫等颜色互相融合的灿烂效果。《稗史汇编》说："瓷有同是一质，遂成异质，同是一色，遂成异色者，水土所合，非人力之巧所能加，是之谓窑变。"清雍正时，唐英在仿古代钧窑的基础上，利用景德镇原料成功地烧造出更加璀璨夺目的窑变釉瓷器。

　　荸荠尊在雍正官窑时期成功地烧造过，有青釉、蓝釉等品种传世。该窑变釉弦纹荸荠尊，造型完全按照雍正的器型制作，如胡惠春先生旧藏的一件雍正粉青釉弦纹荸荠瓶与另外一仵私人珍藏的雍正粉青釉三系弦纹荸荠尊，均与此造型有渊源关系。而该尊窑变红色如燃烧的火焰，给人以釉色雄浑之感，是光绪官窑瓷器中难得一见的珍品。

◉ 参考文献

杨静荣主编《故宫博物院藏文物珍品大系—颜色釉》，上海科学技术出版社、香港商务印书馆，1999年，第144页图131。

清道光　斗彩灵芝纹杯

高3.9厘米　口径7.5厘米　足径2.8厘米

Cup with magic fungus design in contrasting colors
Daoguang period, Qing Dynasty
Height: 3.9cm, Diameter of mouth: 7.5cm, Diameter
of foot: 2.8cm

　　杯撇口，深腹，圈足。底青花三行竖书"大清道光年制"款。造
型规整，内壁素白，外壁绘斗彩团灵芝图案，构图简洁大方，色彩鲜
艳典雅。据文献记载，斗彩始于明宣德年间，以成化斗彩声誉最隆。
清乾隆朝朱琰撰《陶说》记："古瓷五彩，成窑为最，其点染生动，有
出于丹青家之上者。画手固高，画料亦精。"

　　清代官窑瓷器继承明代优良传统。自康熙开始就仿成化斗彩品
种，色彩比成化更加丰富。雍正时期斗彩团灵芝杯即是仿得十分成功
的一个品种，但雍正以后，便很少生产。这件道光灵芝纹斗彩杯，在
传世品中极为罕见。该碗造型玲珑精巧，胎体轻薄，釉质温润，外壁
所绘之花卉图案，布局疏朗，具雍正官窑神韵。

◎ 参考文献

王莉英主编《故宫博物院藏文物珍品大系—五彩·斗彩》（上）·上海科学技术出版社·香港商务印书馆·1999年·第199页图181·第257页图235。

清嘉庆、道光　五彩题诗十月芙蓉花神杯（两件）

清嘉庆：高4.8厘米　口径5.9厘米　足径2.7厘米

清道光：高5厘米　口径6.6厘米　足径2.5厘米

Polychrome cups with design of flowers of twelve months-hibiscus in October
Jiaqing period, Qing Dynasty
Height: 4.8cm, Diameter of mouth: 5.9cm, Diameter of foot: 2.7cm
Daoguang period, Qing Dynasty
Height: 5cm, Diameter of mouth: 6.6cm, Diameter of foot: 2.5cm

　　杯微撇口，深腹，直圈足。足底一书"大清嘉庆年制"青花篆书款，一书"大清道光年制"青花篆书款。两只杯子书写同一诗句："清香和宿雨，佳色出晴烟。"当是描绘十月芙蓉花的。

　　这个品种是康熙官窑开始生产的，十二个为一套，杯上绘有各种不同的花纹，象征十二个月。其完整成套者，主要收藏于北京故宫博物院。十二月花卉纹杯是宫中的实用器皿，造型工整，构思奇巧，彩绘娴熟，颇受皇帝青睐，但在使用中难免破损，所以康熙以后历代官窑继续生产，一直延续到光绪时期，这两件十月芙蓉花卉纹杯，造型和彩绘与康熙产品一脉相承，难分伯仲，如果没有款识，很难与康熙真品区别。

　　十二月花神杯每杯各绘画一种花，题诗一句，摘录如下：

　　一月水仙花：春风弄玉来清书，夜月凌波上大堤。二月玉兰花：金英翠萼带春寒，黄色花中有几般。

　　三月桃花：风花新社燕，时节旧春浓。四月牡丹花：晓艳远分金掌露，暮香深惹玉堂风。

　　五月石榴花：露色珠帘映，香风粉壁遮。六月荷花：根是泥中玉，心承露下珠。

　　七月兰花：广殿轻香发，高台远吹吟。八月桂花：枝生无限月，花满自然秋。

　　九月菊花：千载白衣酒，一生青女香。十月芙蓉花：清香和宿雨，佳色出晴烟。

　　十一月月季花：不随千种尽，独放一年红。十二月梅花：素艳雪凝树，清香风满枝。

⊙ 参考文献

叶佩兰著《中国彩瓷》，上海古籍出版社，2005年，第170、171页图479。

王莉英主编《故宫博物院藏文物珍品大系——五彩·斗彩》，上海科学技术出版社，香港商务印书馆，1999年，第152、153页图140。

　　碗深弧壁，敞口，圈足，为典型的宫廷膳碗造型。外壁以柠檬黄彩为地，锥刻细密流畅的轧道卷草纹，其间中心有三个团型开光，内各绘一羊，是典型的吉祥图案，取谐音寓意《易经》泰卦，象征万物同春、诸事如意。圈足内红彩竖书双行"大清咸丰年制"六字楷书款。

　　咸丰皇帝清文宗奕詝在位11年，其间战事多难，太平军于咸丰四年（1854年）占领景德镇，一把大火烧毁了御窑厂；英法联军一把大火又烧毁了圆明园，存放于园中的官窑瓷器损失殆尽。故咸丰官窑瓷器存世量极为稀少，成为收藏家追逐的目标。

　　此碗是宫廷的实用器皿，俗称"膳碗"。洋彩色地轧道开光膳碗是创烧于乾隆早期的名贵宫廷专用品，在嘉道时期大量制作，该碗的艺术风格与嘉庆道光时期的官窑如出一辙。北京故宫博物院珍藏一件尺寸较小的同类咸丰开光膳碗，开光内画博古纹，可与本件三羊碗比较，尤其是款识的笔法极为相似，当出自同一人手。而该三羊碗尺寸比故宫的那件还大，且纹饰主题内容更显丰富生动。

大清咸
豐年製

⊙ 参考文献

叶佩兰主编《故宫博物院藏文物珍品大系——珐琅彩·粉彩》，上海科学技术出版社、香港商务印书馆，1999年，第256页。

故宫博物院编、耿宝昌主编《孙瀛洲的陶瓷世界》，紫禁城出版社，2005年，第330、331页，图208。

口微撇，圈足。碗外壁绘四组折枝花卉，以鲜艳的红彩绘制四朵小花，并配以浅淡的青花花叶，构图雅致秀美。底圈足内青花书"大清光绪年制"双行六字楷书款。

此种小碗雍正、乾隆、嘉庆、道光均有制作，传世品较多，胎体轻薄，色彩上乾隆以后作品比明代、雍正时浓重，碗底均有各朝代年代款。青花红彩明成化、弘治、正德时期传世品虽然不多，但都很精致，有的器物还成为后代的摹本。此对小杯就是清光绪仿明式风格烧制的典型官窑产品。

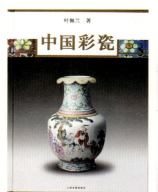

参考文献

叶佩兰著《中国彩瓷》，上海古籍出版社，2005年，第165页、92页图207。

清道光、同治　仿明式青花内夕寒二友外庭院仕女盘（两件）

清同治：高3.8厘米　口径17.6厘米　足径11厘米

清道光：高4厘米　口径18.2厘米　足径11.5厘米

Blue and white plates with pine-bamboo-plum design
Daoguang period, Qing Dynasty
Height: 4, Diameter of mouth: 18.2, Diameter of foot: 11.5cm
Tongzhi period, Qing Dynasty
Height: 3.8cm, Diameter of mouth: 17.6cm, Diameter of foot: 11cm

撇口，弧腹，宽圈足。造型规整，胎体轻薄。通体施白釉，
光洁莹润。外壁绘青花人物故事图案，楼阁栏杆，山石盆景，
枝叶芙蓉，人物于其间神态盎然。盘内绘青花松竹梅纹饰，枝干皴
裂，松枝繁茂，梅花或含苞待放或盛开枝头，竹子秀气挺拔，根
端土石交杂，小草蔓生，给人以生机勃勃之感。足底分别书写
"大清道光年制"六字三行青花篆书款和"大清同治年制"六字
双行楷书款。两件盘形制相似，纹饰题材相同，绘画风格各异，
青花色泽不一，前者浅淡明快，后者浓艳典雅，可以看出道光、
同治两朝瓷器的不同特征。

⊙ **参考文献**

钱振宗主编 《清代瓷器赏鉴》，

上海科技出版社，2005年，第259

页，图342。

24 清光绪　霁蓝釉玉壶春瓶
高28.5厘米　口径9.5厘米　足径11.5厘米
Pear-shaped vase in sky-clearing blue glaze
Guangxu period, Qing Dynasty
Height: 28.5cm, Diameter of mouth: 9.5cm,
Diameter of foot: 11.5cm

　　瓶敞口外撇，短颈，溜肩，鼓腹，圈足。底部蓝釉下书青花"大清光绪年制"双行六字楷书款。霁蓝釉色浅淡，蓝中泛微白。

　　玉壶春瓶又叫玉壶春壶，是宋代流行的酒器，宋以后历代各地窑场均有烧制，到清代酒器功能消失，逐渐演变成陈设用具。

　　霁蓝釉是景德镇窑创烧的一种高温钴蓝釉，自元代问世后，历经明、清各朝盛烧不衰。据记载，霁蓝釉瓷器自明以来多是朝廷祭天的用具，造型规整、釉色纯正，从传世实物看，各朝的霁蓝釉呈色有细微的变化，但总体风格给人以庄严肃穆之感。

⊙ 参考文献

钱振宗 主编《清代瓷器赏鉴》，上海科学技术出版社，2005年，第265页图351。

该盘运用了多种复杂而新颖的釉彩装饰手法，呈现出严谨细致、富丽堂皇的宫廷艺术风格。

盘背面描绘的是传统的中国纹样，与前述的珊瑚红地金彩宝相花小碗完全一样，在深沉浓郁的珊瑚红地上以明亮的金彩描绘缠枝宝相莲花与绶带宝罄一匝，寓意吉祥喜庆，金红相映，鲜艳而热烈，倍增艺术装饰效果。

盘内则使用了富有西洋巴洛克风格的装饰纹样与配色方案，与背面的传统纹饰形成了强烈对比。盘心的团花图案结构以放射状层层铺排，花卉的花头也采用了西洋透视法进行细致的渲染，形成强烈的立体层次感，以明丽娇艳的松绿釉为色地，使整个画面充满了鲜明的异国风情。

道光时期的官窑制作基本上继承了乾隆、嘉庆的风格手法，种类齐全，以青花和彩瓷为主要品种。该盘做工精细，而且把中国传统与西洋舶来手法融为一体，是道光官窑器中极具收藏和研究价值的彩瓷精品。在已经发表的资料中未发现类似的作品，更显珍贵难得。

◎ 参考文献

耿宝昌、吕成龙主编《故宫博物院藏文物珍品大系—杂釉彩·素三彩》，上海科学技术出版社、香港商务印书馆，2009年，第213、214、216页图171～174。

碗撇口，深腹，圈足。内壁绘青花纹饰，里心为十字玉杵形纹，壁饰八吉祥纹。外胭脂红地轧道粉彩绘缠枝宝相花，四圆形开光内绘博古图。底书青花"大清道光年制"六字三行篆书款。

博古图中绘有吉磬、如意、宝瓶、四季花卉、宝鼎、五谷、灯笼等，是典型的吉祥图案，寓意"五谷丰登"、"四季平安"、"吉庆有余"。

胭脂红地或胭脂水是以金为着色剂的粉红釉，是从外国传入的釉料，创烧于康熙晚期而盛行于雍正、乾隆时期。据台北故宫博物院出版、廖宝秀主编《华丽彩瓷——乾隆洋彩》一书的观点，该对碗应该称瓷胎洋彩，故尤为珍贵。本书还是沿用了传统称谓。

118

⊙ **参考文献**

叶佩兰主编《故宫博物院藏文物珍品大系—珐琅彩·粉彩》，上海科学技术出版社、香港商务印书馆，1999年，第244页图216。

27 清宣统　霁蓝釉壶

高9.3厘米　口径7.5厘米　足径7.4厘米　长18厘米

Teapot in sky-clearing blue glaze
Xuantong period, Qing Dynasty
Height: 9.3cm, Diameter of mouth: 7.5cm,
Diameter of foot: 7.4cm, Length: 18cm

该壶造型规整，釉色纯正，壶的肩部印有暗花，整体釉色呈现浓淡深浅的层次变化，使浓艳深沉的霁蓝釉产生旋律，给人以刚劲活泼之感。壶底施白釉，青花竖书双行楷书"大清宣统年制"六字款，字体遒劲，具有典型的官窑款识特征。

1909 年，年仅 3 岁的溥仪被推上皇帝宝座，改年号宣统，成为中国封建历史上的末代君主。这个朝代仅仅经历了 3 年便为新生的中华民国所代替。在短短的 3 年内，景德镇最后一批官窑瓷在御窑厂内烧造完毕，成为官窑瓷器最后的挽歌。宣统官窑瓷器传世品十分稀少，壶类更为少见，此壶造型及美学风格与前朝官窑一脉相承，而且保存原盖，品相完美，对于研究和收藏更显难能可贵。

大清宣
统年製

碗撇口，弧壁，圈足。通身皆以青花五彩为装饰。外壁绘二龙赶珠，两龙分饰红绿二色，各色花朵枝叶遍布其旁，近口沿处以紫、黄、绿彩绘一周八宝纹。足内青花书六字三行篆书"大清道光年制"款。此类碗是清代宫廷膳碗，始见于康熙朝，后成为官窑经典器形，每朝必烧，两百年间持之以恒，造型、纹样也基本保持不变。

五彩瓷起源可追溯到金代磁州窑的红绿彩，景德镇元末明初开始烧造，到明嘉靖、万历时期盛行一时，以色彩丰富、风格刚健著称于世。康熙时期继续生产，主要用于外销。雍、乾以后的五彩适当吸收了粉彩部分原料，尤其是官窑五彩作品，胎质洁白细腻，修饰工整，彩绘技法娴熟。本碗的红绿彩是典型的五彩颜料，没有浓淡深浅的层次变化，给人以刚劲挺拔之感，用以装饰龙纹，体现皇家威严，可谓是事半功倍、相得益彰。高温的青花再低温彩绘，更可看出官窑瓷器不惜工本、追求完美的审美情趣。

◎ **参考文献**

王莉英主编《故宫博物院藏文物珍品大系—五彩·斗彩》，上海科学技术出版社，香港商务印书馆，1999年，第172页图158。

29 民国 粉彩描金开光如意吉祥渣斗（一对）

高8.8厘米 口径8.4厘米 足径5.1厘米

A pair of refuse-vessels with design of auspicious within
reserved panels in famille rose
Republic period
Height: 8.8cm, Diameter of mouth: 8.4cm, Diameter of foot:
5.1cm

渣斗口外撇，宽沿，深腹，形如尊。口沿处彩绘寿桃、蝙蝠、蚱蜢、牡丹花卉，腹身彩绘吉祥如意纹和含苞待放的荷花，并在青花四开光内用金彩书写吉祥如意字样。底书"大清光绪年制"双行六字青花楷书款。其典雅华贵和款识之逼真，俨然光绪本朝之作。

渣斗，又名爹斗、唾壶，用于盛装唾吐物。如置于餐桌，专用于盛载肉骨、鱼刺等食物渣滓，小型者亦用于盛载茶渣，故也列于茶具之中。渣斗在晋代开始使用，瓷质的较常见，比如青瓷渣斗。宋代许多窑厂都烧制渣斗，北宋越窑、耀州窑、南宋官窑等出品都很著名。明、清时景德镇窑也有制作，有多种色釉和彩绘装饰。

明清两代渣斗也被放置于床边和几案上，以备存纳微小废弃之物，用途有所拓宽，材质也日渐多样。有银器或漆器，堪与名窑瓷器媲美。

清嘉庆　粉彩描金缠枝宝相花纹水丞

高3.9厘米　口径3.5厘米　足径5.2厘米

Water container with famille rose decoration of composite
flowers
Jiaqing period, Qing Dynasty
Height: 3.9cm, Diameter of mouth: 3.5cm, Diameter of
foot: 5.2cm

　　水丞扁圆腹，顶开小圆口，平底，浅挖圈足，造型精巧，充满文人雅琪之感。外壁绘粉彩缠枝宝相花，疏朗流畅，敷彩细致鲜明。底足施白釉，书矾红彩"大清嘉庆年制"三行六字篆书款。

　　缠枝宝相花是清代官窑瓷器上最经典的纹样之一，连续不断的曼妙花枝象征绵绵悠长的幸福，而富有色彩质感与表现能力的粉彩也正好适合绘写姿态各异的枝叶花朵，所以缠枝宝相花成为清代瓷器上最常用的纹饰。这件造型简单优美的水丞，虽然尺寸较小，但画师绘写的手法依然细致入微，花头、花蕾、枝蔓均舒展有致、繁而不乱、设色讲究，把粉彩的特点发挥得淋漓尽致，显得玲珑华美，把华贵高雅的宫廷艺术风格表露无遗。

　　这件精美的水丞，是嘉庆时期的官窑精品，传世品中尚未发现类似的嘉庆作品。而且其传承有序，最早为仇焱之珍藏，后有三次苏富比与佳士得拍卖记录。

⊙ **参考文献**

Christie's New York 2007-03-22 Lot 421，
纽约佳士得拍卖，2007 年 3 月 22 日，第 421 号。

Sotheby's Hong Kong 1995-05-04 Lot 158，
香港苏富比拍卖，1995 年 5 月 4 日，第 158 号。

Sotheby's Hong Kong 1994-05-04 Lot 240，
香港苏富比拍卖，1994 年 5 月 4 日，第 240 号。

E.T.Chow Collection 仇焱之旧藏。

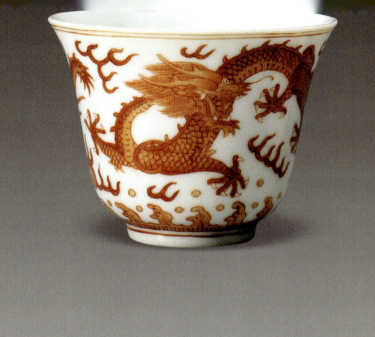

⊙ 参考文献

《中国陶瓷全集》第15卷清
（下），上海人民美术出版社，
2000年，第195页图192。

清光绪　黄地粉彩开光龙凤福寿纹大赏瓶

高 55.8厘米　口径 15.5厘米　足径19厘米

Large vase with famille rose decoration of dragon and phoenix within
reserved panels over a yellow ground
Guangxu period, Qing Dynasty
Height: 55.8cm, Diameter of mouth: 15.5cm, Diameter of foot: 19cm

　　瓶直颈，口外撇，圆腹，圈足。此种造型也称赏瓶，多以青花装饰，是皇帝赏赐大臣的专用器皿。该瓶造型挺拔硕大，外壁施黄釉为地，口沿绘如意云头纹，瓶颈描绘云蝠纹，肩部白色地上绘花蝶寿字纹，腹部绘福寿纹，并有三组圆形开光，内绘龙凤纹，寓意龙凤呈祥。足底双行竖书六字红色楷书"大清光绪年制"款。整体画面饱满，构图规范，彩绘工整，技法娴熟，全器纹饰繁缛，祥瑞之象极多，色彩丰富，艳丽华美，为典型光绪官窑粉彩大器。

　　此粉彩赏瓶，比常见青花赏瓶造型硕大，既给人以大气磅礴之感又与大清帝国烈士暮年的时代风格辉映成趣。

大清光
緒年
製

本书收录瓷器

科技检测报告书

Report of Scientific Verification

北京中陶古艺术品鉴定技术开发中心
Zhongtao Development Center Of Ancient Art Appraisal Technique
地址:北京市朝阳区东三环南路 17 号京瑞大厦 B 座 12C　邮编:100021
Web:www.wwjd.com.cn　电话:010-65810687　传真:010-65833007

检测报告书

检测物品编号:2011011302

检测物品名称:矾红彩描金云龙纹镫

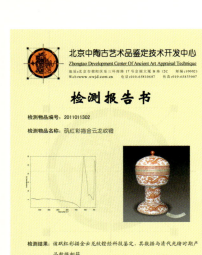

检测结果:该矾红彩描金云龙纹镫经科技鉴定,其数据与清代光绪时期产品数据相符。

北京中陶古艺术品鉴定技术开发中心

鉴定日期:2011 年 1 月 13 日

北京中陶古艺术品鉴定技术开发中心
Zhongtao Development Center Of Ancient Art Appraisal Technique
地址:北京市朝阳区东三环南路 17 号京瑞大厦 B 座 12C　邮编:100021
Web:www.wwjd.com.cn　电话:010-65810687　传真:010-65833007

检测报告书

检测物品编号:2011012408

检测物品名称:斗彩团花纹撇口碗

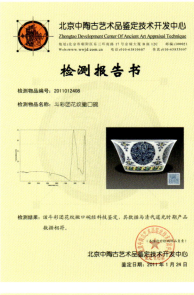

检测结果:该斗彩团花纹撇口碗经科技鉴定,其数据与清代光绪时期产品数据相符。

北京中陶古艺术品鉴定技术开发中心

鉴定日期:2011 年 1 月 24 日

北京中陶古艺术品鉴定技术开发中心
Zhongtao Development Center Of Ancient Art Appraisal Technique
地址:北京市朝阳区东三环南路 17 号京瑞大厦 B 座 12C　邮编:100021
Web:www.wwjd.com.cn　电话:010-65810687　传真:010-65833007

检测报告书

检测物品编号:2011011310

检测物品名称:青花云龙纹盘

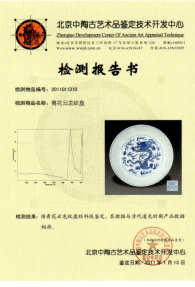

检测结果:该青花云龙纹盘经科技鉴定,其数据与清代道光时期产品数据相符。

北京中陶古艺术品鉴定技术开发中心

鉴定日期:2011 年 1 月 13 日

北京中陶古艺术品鉴定技术开发中心
Zhongtao Development Center Of Ancient Art Appraisal Technique
地址:北京市朝阳区东三环南路 17 号京瑞大厦 B 座 12C　邮编:100021
Web:www.wwjd.com.cn　电话:010-65810687　传真:010-65833007

检测报告书

检测物品编号:2011011313

检测物品名称:洋彩轧道黄地圆光四季山水人物膳碗

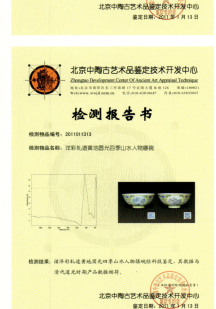

检测结果:该洋彩轧道黄地圆光四季山水人物膳碗经科技鉴定,其数据与清代道光时期产品数据相符。

北京中陶古艺术品鉴定技术开发中心

鉴定日期:2011 年 1 月 13 日

北京中陶古艺术品鉴定技术开发中心
Zhongtao Development Center Of Ancient Art Appraisal Technique
地址:北京市朝阳区东三环南路 17 号京瑞大厦 B 座 12C　邮编:100021
Web:www.wwjd.com.cn　电话:010-65810687　传真:010-65833007

检测报告书

检测物品编号:2011012411

检测物品名称:仿明式青花缠枝花卉纹赏瓶

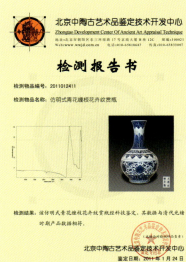

检测结果:该仿明式青花缠枝花卉纹赏瓶经科技鉴定,其数据与清代光绪时期产品数据相符。

北京中陶古艺术品鉴定技术开发中心

鉴定日期:2011 年 1 月 24 日

北京中陶古艺术品鉴定技术开发中心
Zhongtao Development Center Of Ancient Art Appraisal Technique
地址:北京市朝阳区东三环南路 17 号京瑞大厦 B 座 12C　邮编:100021
Web:www.wwjd.com.cn　电话:010-65810687　传真:010-65833007

检测报告书

检测物品编号:2011011311

检测物品名称:斗彩缠枝花卉纹碗 一对

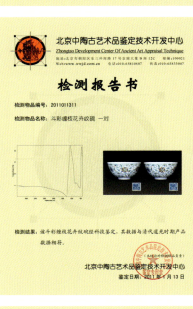

检测结果:该斗彩缠枝花卉纹碗经科技鉴定,其数据与清代道光时期产品数据相符。

北京中陶古艺术品鉴定技术开发中心

鉴定日期:2011 年 1 月 13 日

北京中陶古艺术品鉴定技术开发中心
Zhongtao Development Center Of Ancient Art Appraisal Technique
地址:北京市朝阳区东三环南路 17 号京瑞大厦 B 座 12C　邮编:100021
Web:www.wwjd.com.cn　电话:010-65810687　传真:010-65833007

检测报告书

检测物品编号:2011011315

检测物品名称:珊瑚红地金彩绘缠枝宝相花纹碗

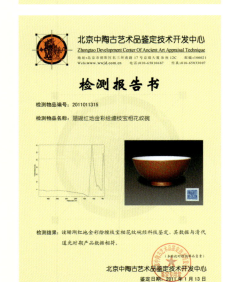

检测结果:该珊瑚红地金彩绘缠枝宝相花纹碗经科技鉴定,其数据与清代道光时期产品数据相符。

北京中陶古艺术品鉴定技术开发中心

鉴定日期:2011 年 1 月 13 日

北京中陶古艺术品鉴定技术开发中心
Zhongtao Development Center Of Ancient Art Appraisal Technique
地址:北京市朝阳区东三环南路 17 号京瑞大厦 B 座 12C　邮编:100021
Web:www.wwjd.com.cn　电话:010-65810687　传真:010-65833007

检测报告书

检测物品编号:2011011314

检测物品名称:珐琅彩题诗耋耄图小瓶

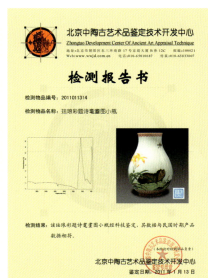

检测结果:该珐琅彩题诗耋耄图小瓶经科技鉴定,其数据与民国时期产品数据相符。

北京中陶古艺术品鉴定技术开发中心

鉴定日期:2011 年 1 月 13 日

北京中陶古艺术品鉴定技术开发中心
Zhongtao Development Center Of Ancient Art Appraisal Technique
地址:北京市朝阳区东三环南路 17 号京瑞大厦 B 座 12C　邮编:100021
Web:www.wwjd.com.cn　电话:010-65810687　传真:010-65833007

检测报告书

检测物品编号:2011011309

检测物品名称:珐琅彩虞美人图题诗瓶 一对

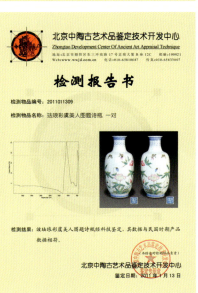

检测结果:该珐琅彩虞美人图题诗瓶经科技鉴定,其数据与民国时期产品数据相符。

北京中陶古艺术品鉴定技术开发中心

鉴定日期:2011 年 1 月 13 日

北京中陶古艺术品鉴定技术开发中心
Zhongtao Development Center Of Ancient Art Appraisal Technique
地址:北京市朝阳区东三环南路17号京瑞大厦B座12C 邮编:100021
Web:www.wwjd.com.cn 电话:010-65810687 传真:010-65833007

检测报告书

检测物品编号: 2011011308

检测物品名称: 彩绘折枝玉兰翠竹纹题诗马蹄杯

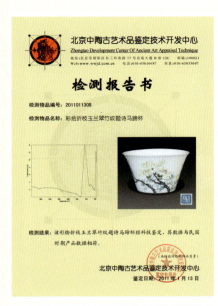

检测结果: 该彩绘折枝玉兰翠竹纹题诗马蹄杯经科技鉴定,其数据与民国时期产品数据相符。

北京中陶古艺术品鉴定技术开发中心
鉴定日期: 2011年1月13日

北京中陶古艺术品鉴定技术开发中心
Zhongtao Development Center Of Ancient Art Appraisal Technique
地址:北京市朝阳区东三环南路17号京瑞大厦B座12C 邮编:100021
Web:www.wwjd.com.cn 电话:010-65810687 传真:010-65833007

检测报告书

检测物品编号: 2011011306

检测物品名称: 窑变釉六棱石榴尊

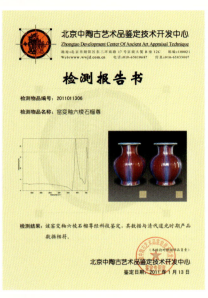

检测结果: 该窑变釉六棱石榴尊经科技鉴定,其数据与清代道光时期产品数据相符。

北京中陶古艺术品鉴定技术开发中心
鉴定日期: 2011年1月13日

北京中陶古艺术品鉴定技术开发中心
Zhongtao Development Center Of Ancient Art Appraisal Technique
地址:北京市朝阳区东三环南路17号京瑞大厦B座12C 邮编:100021
Web:www.wwjd.com.cn 电话:010-65810687 传真:010-65833007

检测报告书

检测物品编号: 2011011318

检测物品名称: 粉彩花鸟纹撇口碗 一对

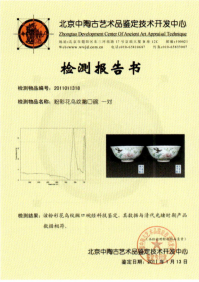

检测结果: 该粉彩花鸟纹撇口碗经科技鉴定,其数据与清代光绪时期产品数据相符。

北京中陶古艺术品鉴定技术开发中心
鉴定日期: 2011年1月13日

北京中陶古艺术品鉴定技术开发中心
Zhongtao Development Center Of Ancient Art Appraisal Technique
地址:北京市朝阳区东三环南路17号京瑞大厦B座12C 邮编:100021
Web:www.wwjd.com.cn 电话:010-65810687 传真:010-65833007

检测报告书

检测物品编号: 2011012409

检测物品名称: 绿彩龙纹盘

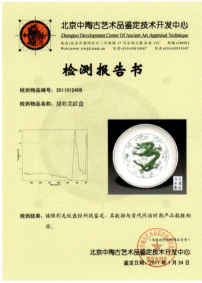

检测结果: 该绿彩龙纹盘经科技鉴定,其数据与清代同治时期产品数据相符。

北京中陶古艺术品鉴定技术开发中心
鉴定日期: 2011年1月24日

北京中陶古艺术品鉴定技术开发中心
Zhongtao Development Center Of Ancient Art Appraisal Technique
地址:北京市朝阳区东三环南路17号京瑞大厦B座12C 邮编:100021
Web:www.wwjd.com.cn 电话:010-65810687 传真:010-65833007

检测报告书

检测物品编号: 2011012410

检测物品名称: 霁蓝釉琮式象耳方尊

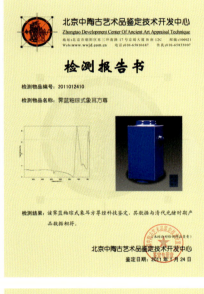

检测结果: 该霁蓝釉琮式象耳方尊经科技鉴定,其数据与清代光绪时期产品数据相符。

北京中陶古艺术品鉴定技术开发中心
鉴定日期: 2011年1月24日

北京中陶古艺术品鉴定技术开发中心
Zhongtao Development Center Of Ancient Art Appraisal Technique
地址:北京市朝阳区东三环南路17号京瑞大厦B座12C 邮编:100021
Web:www.wwjd.com.cn 电话:010-65810687 传真:010-65833007

检测报告书

检测物品编号: 2011011303

检测物品名称: 天蓝釉小罐

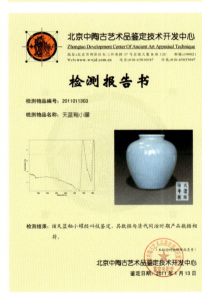

检测结果: 该天蓝釉小罐经科技鉴定,其数据与清代同治时期产品数据相符。

北京中陶古艺术品鉴定技术开发中心
鉴定日期: 2011年1月13日

北京中陶古艺术品鉴定技术开发中心
Zhongtao Development Center Of Ancient Art Appraisal Technique
地址:北京市朝阳区东三环南路17号京瑞大厦B座12C 邮编:100021
Web:www.wwjd.com.cn 电话:010-65810687 传真:010-65833007

检测报告书

检测物品编号: 2011012404

检测物品名称: 黄釉暗刻云龙纹盘 一对

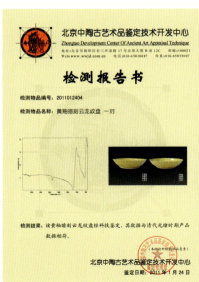

检测结果: 该黄釉暗刻云龙纹盘经科技鉴定,其数据与清代光绪时期产品数据相符。

北京中陶古艺术品鉴定技术开发中心
鉴定日期: 2011年1月24日

北京中陶古艺术品鉴定技术开发中心
Zhongtao Development Center Of Ancient Art Appraisal Technique
地址:北京市朝阳区东三环南路17号京瑞大厦B座12C 邮编:100021
Web:www.wwjd.com.cn 电话:010-65810687 传真:010-65833007

检测报告书

检测物品编号: 2011011316

检测物品名称: 豆青釉划花团花纹碗

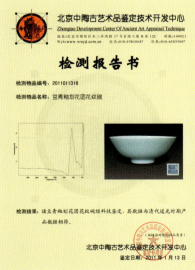

检测结果: 该豆青釉划花团花纹碗经科技鉴定,其数据与清代道光时期产品数据相符。

北京中陶古艺术品鉴定技术开发中心
鉴定日期: 2011年1月13日

北京中陶古艺术品鉴定技术开发中心
Zhongtao Development Center Of Ancient Art Appraisal Technique
地址:北京市朝阳区东三环南路17号京瑞大厦B座12C 邮编:100021
Web:www.wwjd.com.cn 电话:010-65810687 传真:010-65833007

检测报告书

检测物品编号: 2011011319

检测物品名称: 窑变火焰红釉弦纹尊

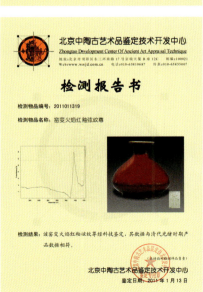

检测结果: 该窑变火焰红釉弦纹尊经科技鉴定,其数据与清代光绪时期产品数据相符。

北京中陶古艺术品鉴定技术开发中心
鉴定日期: 2011年1月13日

北京中陶古艺术品鉴定技术开发中心
Zhongtao Development Center Of Ancient Art Appraisal Technique
地址:北京市朝阳区东三环商路 17 号京瑞大厦 B 座 12C 邮编:100021
Web:www.wwjd.com.cn 电话:010-65810687 传真:010-65833007

检测报告书

检测物品编号: 2011011304

检测物品名称: 仿成化斗彩团灵芝纹小杯

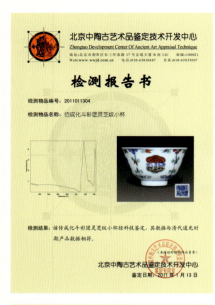

检测结果: 该仿成化斗彩团灵芝纹小杯经科技鉴定，其数据与清代道光时期产品数据相符。

北京中陶古艺术品鉴定技术开发中心

鉴定日期: 2011 年 1 月 13 日

北京中陶古艺术品鉴定技术开发中心
Zhongtao Development Center Of Ancient Art Appraisal Technique
地址:北京市朝阳区东三环商路 17 号京瑞大厦 B 座 12C 邮编:100021
Web:www.wwjd.com.cn 电话:010-65810687 传真:010-65833007

检测报告书

检测物品编号: 2011011322

检测物品名称: 五彩题诗十月芙蓉花神杯 一对

检测结果: 该五彩题诗十月芙蓉花神杯经科技鉴定，其数据分别与清代嘉庆、道光时期产品数据相符。

北京中陶古艺术品鉴定技术开发中心

鉴定日期: 2011 年 1 月 13 日

北京中陶古艺术品鉴定技术开发中心
Zhongtao Development Center Of Ancient Art Appraisal Technique
地址:北京市朝阳区东三环商路 17 号京瑞大厦 B 座 12C 邮编:100021
Web:www.wwjd.com.cn 电话:010-65810687 传真:010-65833007

检测报告书

检测物品编号: 2011030306

检测物品名称: 黄地轧道粉彩圆光三阳开泰纹碗

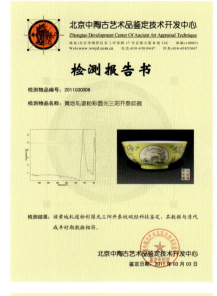

检测结果: 该黄地轧道粉彩圆光三阳开泰纹碗经科技鉴定，其数据与清代咸丰时期数据相符。

北京中陶古艺术品鉴定技术开发中心

鉴定日期: 2011 年 03 月 03 日

北京中陶古艺术品鉴定技术开发中心
Zhongtao Development Center Of Ancient Art Appraisal Technique
地址:北京市朝阳区东三环商路 17 号京瑞大厦 B 座 12C 邮编:100021
Web:www.wwjd.com.cn 电话:010-65810687 传真:010-65833007

检测报告书

检测物品编号: 2011011321

检测物品名称: 仿明式青花描红折枝忍冬纹小杯 一对

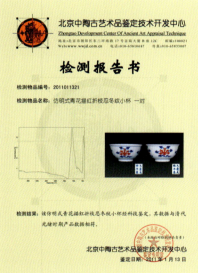

检测结果: 该仿明式青花描红折枝忍冬纹小杯经科技鉴定，其数据与清代光绪时期产品数据相符。

北京中陶古艺术品鉴定技术开发中心

鉴定日期: 2011 年 1 月 13 日

北京中陶古艺术品鉴定技术开发中心
Zhongtao Development Center Of Ancient Art Appraisal Technique
地址:北京市朝阳区东三环商路 17 号京瑞大厦 B 座 12C 邮编:100021
Web:www.wwjd.com.cn 电话:010-65810687 传真:010-65833007

检测报告书

检测物品编号: 2011011307

检测物品名称: 仿明式内岁寒三友纹外庭院仕女图盘

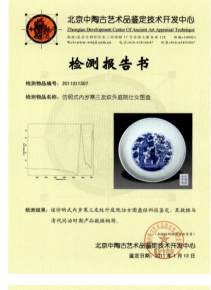

检测结果: 该仿明式内岁寒三友纹外庭院仕女图盘经科技鉴定，其数据与清代同治时期产品数据相符。

北京中陶古艺术品鉴定技术开发中心

鉴定日期: 2011 年 1 月 13 日

北京中陶古艺术品鉴定技术开发中心
Zhongtao Development Center Of Ancient Art Appraisal Technique
地址:北京市朝阳区东三环商路 17 号京瑞大厦 B 座 12C 邮编:100021
Web:www.wwjd.com.cn 电话:010-65810687 传真:010-65833007

检测报告书

检测物品编号: 2010123010

检测物品名称: 仿明式内岁寒三友纹外庭院仕女图盘

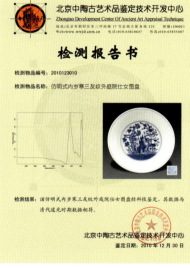

检测结果: 该仿明式内岁寒三友纹外庭院仕女图盘经科技鉴定，其数据与清代道光时期数据相符。

北京中陶古艺术品鉴定技术开发中心

鉴定日期: 2010 年 12 月 30 日

北京中陶古艺术品鉴定技术开发中心
Zhongtao Development Center Of Ancient Art Appraisal Technique
地址:北京市朝阳区东三环商路 17 号京瑞大厦 B 座 12C 邮编:100021
Web:www.wwjd.com.cn 电话:010-65810687 传真:010-65833007

检测报告书

检测物品编号: 2011011305

检测物品名称: 霁蓝釉玉壶春瓶

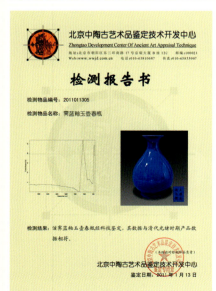

检测结果: 该霁蓝釉玉壶春瓶经科技鉴定，其数据与清代光绪时期产品数据相符。

北京中陶古艺术品鉴定技术开发中心

鉴定日期: 2011 年 1 月 13 日

北京中陶古艺术品鉴定技术开发中心
Zhongtao Development Center Of Ancient Art Appraisal Technique
地址:北京市朝阳区东三环商路 17 号京瑞大厦 B 座 12C 邮编:100021
Web:www.wwjd.com.cn 电话:010-65810687 传真:010-65833007

检测报告书

检测物品编号: 2011011312

检测物品名称: 外珊瑚红地描金缠枝宝相花内松石绿地粉彩宝相花纹盘

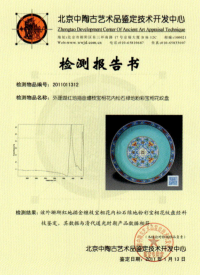

检测结果: 该外珊瑚红地描金缠枝宝相花内松石绿地粉彩宝相花纹盘经科技鉴定，其数据与清代道光时期产品数据相符。

北京中陶古艺术品鉴定技术开发中心

鉴定日期: 2011 年 1 月 13 日

北京中陶古艺术品鉴定技术开发中心
Zhongtao Development Center Of Ancient Art Appraisal Technique
地址:北京市朝阳区东三环商路 17 号京瑞大厦 B 座 12C 邮编:100021
Web:www.wwjd.com.cn 电话:010-65810687 传真:010-65833007

检测报告书

检测物品编号: 2011011317

检测物品名称: 洋彩胭脂红地轧道圆光博古图膳碗 一对

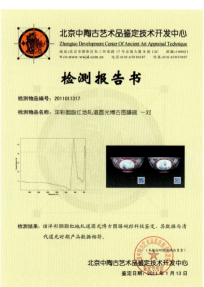

检测结果: 该洋彩胭脂红地轧道圆光博古图膳碗经科技鉴定，其数据与清代道光时期产品数据相符。

北京中陶古艺术品鉴定技术开发中心

鉴定日期: 2011 年 1 月 13 日

北京中陶古艺术品鉴定技术开发中心
Zhongtao Development Center Of Ancient Art Appraisal Technique
地址:北京市朝阳区东三环南路 17 号京瑞大厦 B 座 12C　邮编:100021
Web:www.wwjd.com.cn　电话:010-65810687　传真:010-65833007

检测报告书

检测物品编号: 2011032101

检测物品名称: 清宣统款霁蓝釉执壶

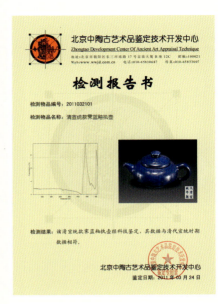

检测结果: 该清宣统款霁蓝釉执壶经科技鉴定, 其数据与清代宣统时期数据相符。

北京中陶古艺术品鉴定技术开发中心

鉴定日期: 2011 年 03 月 24 日

北京中陶古艺术品鉴定技术开发中心
Zhongtao Development Center Of Ancient Art Appraisal Technique
地址:北京市朝阳区东三环南路 17 号京瑞大厦 B 座 12C　邮编:100021
Web:www.wwjd.com.cn　电话:010-65810687　传真:010-65833007

检测报告书

检测物品编号: 2011012405

检测物品名称: 五彩穿花龙凤呈祥纹大婚碗 一对

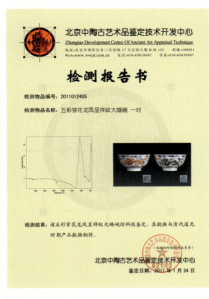

检测结果: 该五彩穿花龙凤呈祥纹大婚碗经科技鉴定, 其数据与清代道光时期产品数据相符。

北京中陶古艺术品鉴定技术开发中心

鉴定日期: 2011 年 1 月 24 日

北京中陶古艺术品鉴定技术开发中心
Zhongtao Development Center Of Ancient Art Appraisal Technique
地址:北京市朝阳区东三环南路 17 号京瑞大厦 B 座 12C　邮编:100021
Web:www.wwjd.com.cn　电话:010-65810687　传真:010-65833007

检测报告书

检测物品编号: 2011011320

检测物品名称: 粉彩描金开光如意吉祥小渣斗 一对

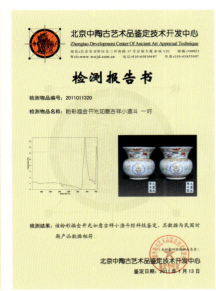

检测结果: 该粉彩描金开光如意吉祥小渣斗经科技鉴定, 其数据与民国时期产品数据相符。

北京中陶古艺术品鉴定技术开发中心

鉴定日期: 2011 年 1 月 13 日

北京中陶古艺术品鉴定技术开发中心
Zhongtao Development Center Of Ancient Art Appraisal Technique
地址:北京市朝阳区东三环南路 17 号京瑞大厦 B 座 12C　邮编:100021
Web:www.wwjd.com.cn　电话:010-65810687　传真:010-65833007

检测报告书

检测物品编号: 2011042401

检测物品名称: 粉彩描金缠枝宝相花纹水丞

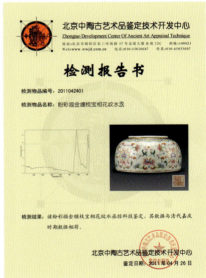

检测结果: 该粉彩描金缠枝宝相花纹水丞经科技鉴定, 其数据与清代嘉庆时期数据相符。

北京中陶古艺术品鉴定技术开发中心

鉴定日期: 2011 年 04 月 26 日

北京中陶古艺术品鉴定技术开发中心
Zhongtao Development Center Of Ancient Art Appraisal Technique
地址:北京市朝阳区东三环南路 17 号京瑞大厦 B 座 12C　邮编:100021
Web:www.wwjd.com.cn　电话:010-65810687　传真:010-65833007

检测报告书

检测物品编号: 2011012402

检测物品名称: 矾红彩云龙纹杯 一对

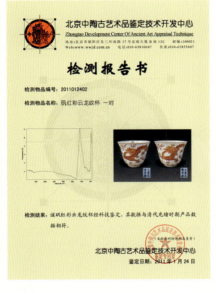

检测结果: 该矾红彩云龙纹杯经科技鉴定, 其数据与清代光绪时期产品数据相符。

北京中陶古艺术品鉴定技术开发中心

鉴定日期: 2011 年 1 月 24 日

北京中陶古艺术品鉴定技术开发中心
Zhongtao Development Center Of Ancient Art Appraisal Technique
地址:北京市朝阳区东三环南路 17 号京瑞大厦 B 座 12C　邮编:100021
Web:www.wwjd.com.cn　电话:010-65810687　传真:010-65833007

检测报告书

检测物品编号: 2011052407

检测物品名称: 光绪粉彩开光龙凤纹赏瓶

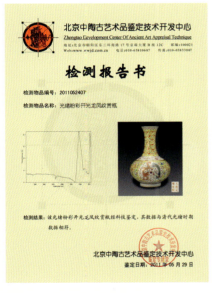

检测结果: 该光绪粉彩开光龙凤纹赏瓶经科技鉴定, 其数据与清代光绪时期数据相符。

北京中陶古艺术品鉴定技术开发中心

鉴定日期: 2011 年 05 月 29 日

专论

Monograph

晚清至民国景德镇彩瓷的鉴赏

叶佩兰

回顾几千年的历史，中国古陶瓷在每一个历史阶段都演绎着不同时代风格的艺术品，成为我们的文化宝藏，并在世界上享有极高的声誉。

清代瓷器尤其前三朝的制作水平达到登峰造极，但清代后期据有关史料记载，由于国力的不足，在嘉庆年间宫廷曾下令停止过官窑的烧造，可是到晚清时期官窑的制瓷技术仍然保存着，无论是青花、粉彩、颜色釉等方面都有所发展和创新。如光绪时期创造的浅绛彩，同治光绪时期独特的官窑粉彩以及王炳荣、陈国治的雕瓷、李治元的素烧反瓷，民国时期的仿雍乾珐琅彩等，都是突破了历代的制瓷成就。正如晚清著名瓷书《陶雅》（陈浏著）中所说"乾隆初年，去雍未远，倡条冶业，不乏奇丽之观。中叶以后，深厚固不如康熙，美丽也不及雍正，惟以不惜工本之故，犹足以容与中流。嘉道以降，画工彩料，直愈趋愈下，而极精之品，犹自有不可埋没处"。

一　浅绛彩瓷的出现

浅绛彩瓷是清代晚期至民国早期较为流行的一个民窑釉上彩瓷器。从器表、纹饰上看，件件犹如一幅中国水墨画小品。瓷器色彩浅淡，有淡赭、淡蓝、水绿、草绿，再点缀紫、红等多种色彩渲染而成，清淡幽雅。因画面突出淡赭的使用，有人借用国画中"浅绛"一词，将此种瓷画称为"浅绛彩"。综观这类彩瓷也不一定都突出浅赭色，有的突出淡绿色，有的突出淡蓝、淡灰色，瓷画仿佛工笔水彩，所以有的学者将浅绛彩类的瓷器又称为"水墨五彩"，也是很有见地的。

浅绛彩实际上是在粉彩基础上，进一步演变出来的一种彩瓷。与粉彩相比它的特点是：彩料中含粉质较多，施彩较薄，显得色彩浅淡。由于施彩时不用玻璃白打底，或彩面也不盖"雪白"，因此画面色彩不光亮，常常见有彩磨或剥彩现象，影响器物的外观美。其地釉属青白釉，釉面有的不平，有波浪感，宣统与民国早期者地釉较白。

在纹饰方面，主要是山水风景、人物故事、花鸟、博古图等。绘画时绘瓷人采用了文人画的某些技法，据《景德镇近代陶人录》一书介绍，绘制浅绛彩的艺人，都有较高的文化素养，善于绘画又善于书法。在绘画上也是多方面的能手，山水、人物、花鸟、鱼虫都能画，从图稿设计到勾画渲染皆由一人完成。绘画题材多采用元代以来的文人画稿，因此与宣统的官窑粉彩比较起来，画面显得自由豪放。同时还结合绘画内容在空白处墨书相应诗句，有四言、五言或七言诗，诗文后题写绘画的时间、地点和作者姓名，绘画时间一般用干支表示，达到诗、书、画融为一体的艺术效果。浅绛彩是近代彩瓷的新品种。

浅绛彩瓷器，社会上流传较多，据有关文献记载当时出现了一些绘浅绛彩的名家，最

1．民国浅绛彩米芾拜石图瓷板：曾美芳主编《景德镇彩瓷三百年》，江西美术出版社，2003年，图57。

2．同治粉彩折枝花卉圆盒：叶佩兰主编《故宫博物院藏文物珍品大系——珐琅彩·粉彩》，上海科学技术出版社，香港商务印书馆，1999年，第259页图230。

著名的是程门及其长子程言、金品卿、汪有棠、汪少维等，在19世纪末至20世纪初期影响很大，从社会上流散的浅绛彩瓷来看，绘画能手辈出，许多作画者名不见经传。据《景德镇史稿》介绍，浅绛彩瓷入民国以后逐渐失传。

浅绛彩瓷器的造型主要是陈设品和生活用品。在陈设品中有瓷画板及各式瓶如双耳瓶、琮式瓶、洗口棒槌瓶、四方撇口瓶等。还有形式多样的帽筒如圆形、四方形、圆形挖孔式或六方形挖孔式，既作陈设又能实用。笔筒均为晚清时期新出现的小型圆式笔筒，茶具也比较常见，此外还有扁式盖缸、粥罐、折沿洗、香炉等，造型很丰富，证实浅绛彩在当时还是受民间欢迎的。

浅绛彩瓷的款识，一般来说在墨彩题句中已有纪年款了。但在器物的底部也还有红彩篆书"同治"二字或"同治年制"、"光绪年制"的年款，或作画者的堂号。从款识字体及色彩上看为典型晚清民窑彩瓷款识。总之，浅绛彩瓷器是我国陶瓷发展史上晚清至民国初出现的一朵奇葩。

二　独特的同光宣粉彩

从故宫传世品看晚清官窑粉彩瓷器，大部分是御窑厂专门为皇帝和慈禧太后所烧制的餐具和陈设瓷。据史料记载，同治七年皇帝大婚，由江西巡抚景福负责烧制"大婚礼造器"达七千多件。光绪时为慈禧寿辰又烧制了数以万计的色地粉彩瓷器。这些宫廷用瓷，除了少量用冷色地外，大部分以浓重的暖色做地，如大红、大绿、明黄、藕荷色，色彩都较厚润，绘寓意万寿喜庆的花鸟、花卉，题材丰富。同治大婚餐具以明黄为地，绘红蝠金团寿、五蝠捧寿、蝴蝶双喜、梅雀与丛竹等达十多种，都是经过"大内"批准制作的。至今在北京故宫博物院图书馆收藏着当时给皇帝烧制瓷器的画样。

同治白地粉彩瓷器色彩较浅淡，喜绘折枝花卉。此时乾、嘉时常用的色地"开光"装饰已基本停用，仅在皇帝和皇后结婚时的专用粉彩瓷器上才有"开光"龙凤的画面。光绪白地粉彩瓷器，可分精、细两类。精者一般盘碗可与道光粉彩媲美，花卉花鸟纹饰生动，色彩鲜亮，有"大清光绪年制"六字楷书款。粗者分为稍大些的盘、碗、折沿洗等，胎体厚重，色彩浓重、凝厚，龙凤花朵纹饰粗放。光绪喜仿乾隆粉彩九桃大瓶及乾隆粉彩百鹿尊，仿品一般胎体厚重，色彩浓艳，纹饰绘画缺乏立体感。

同治、光绪粉彩中的特殊形体，如：1、同治粉彩灰槽。见《中国彩瓷》图705，器下半部分像长方形洗，洗的后边一面为高出后壁呈云头状的后背，背面及洗的下部三面粉彩绘蝴蝶

3、光绪粉彩描金五伦图象耳瓶：叶佩兰主编《故宫博物院藏文物珍品大系—珐琅彩·粉彩》，上海科学技术出版社，香港商务印书馆，1999年，第266页图236。

4、宣统粉彩玉壶春瓶：叶佩兰主编《故宫博物院藏文物珍品大系—珐琅彩·粉彩》，上海科学技术出版社，香港商务印书馆，1999年，第290页图259。

5. 民国仿珐琅彩高士图（附"陶务监督郭葆昌谨制"款）：叶佩兰著《古瓷辨识》，山东美术出版社，2005年，图59。

草虫，即"探花及第"图案。传说此器是放于炉前接炉灰用的灰槽。2、同治黄底粉彩凸雕三果圆盒。盒面凸雕佛手、石榴和桃，中间一展翅翔蝠为"福寿三多"之意，盒底刻雕名家"王炳荣造"款识，这种雕瓷粉彩为同治所特有。3、赏瓶。是宫廷内赏赐或陈设用品，乾隆以后较多。较为常见的造型为撇口，长颈，肩上凸起一道弦纹，圆腹，底青花或红彩书写朝代款识，此式瓶清宫档案称为"玉堂春瓶"。到清晚期赏瓶式样增多，还有哥釉四方八卦瓶、钧红釉四方杏圆贯耳瓶、厂官釉太极纸槌瓶等多种，光绪还特有青花云蝠直颈扁腹瓶。4、大地瓶，大缸，大花盆。这些大器造型端庄，纹饰绘画精致，牡丹花卉较为突出，色彩鲜艳。光绪大地瓶高达130～150厘米，大花盆高50、口径40～50厘米。不难看出晚清烧制大件器物的水平还是很高的。5、"大雅斋"款的粉彩瓷器。这是光绪时独有的品种。造型有盘、碗、盒、高足盘、高足碗、匙、钵缸、圆盒、花盆、大缸等。纹饰题材多绘藤萝花鸟、葡萄花鸟、鹭鸶莲花等，很有新意。款识书写的方法一般用红彩从右向左粗线条横书"大雅斋"三字款，款旁有红彩龙凤纹组成的椭圆形闲章款，闲章内书"天地一家春"篆字。"天地一家春"为圆明园内一处建筑的名称。据说慈禧为兰贵人时曾住过这里。这种一瓷二款的做法为光绪时所特有。6、秋操纪念杯。光绪年间曾举行过几次秋季军事操练。此种杯为当时操练后的纪念品。见到的有三种形式，一种为粉牡丹花式，一种为绿釉荷叶式，这两种均以叶茎为柄，柄中空与杯相通，又可称为吸杯。在柄的背面墨书操练的时间和地点。还有一种为普通酒杯形式，杯外壁绘云龙纹，口边墨书操练时间和地点。

晚清官窑粉彩款识写法，不同品类的器物书写不同的款识。如一般的官窑制品，器底写青花楷书朝代款。同治大婚时宫内用品器底红彩书写"同治年制"、"长春同庆"、"燕喜同和"等四字款。光绪时的陈设品，底部用红彩书写"永庆长春"款。还有宫内室名款"乐寿堂"、"体和殿"、"长春宫"。慈禧专用的是"大雅斋"和"天地一家春"的组合款。

宣统时期的粉彩。宣统一朝仅三年，景德镇御窑厂虽然仍继续烧造宫廷使用的粉彩瓷器，但从传世品看，宣统的粉彩瓷器都是光绪品种的再出现，只是款识不同而已。较为突出的是粉彩牡丹纹玉壶春瓶，此瓶虽为清末制品，但制作很精致，具有雍正粉彩的韵味，色彩浓淡适宜，纹饰绘画细腻，有层次感，可谓晚清官窑精品。此式瓶在翰海拍卖会上，落槌价达20余万元，不难看出它深受收藏者的青睐。

现代仿制的嘉庆以后各朝粉彩瓷器时有出现，仿制的都是官窑中常见品或名品，如嘉庆款色地粉彩，道光款及"慎德堂制"款粉彩，同治、光绪、宣统款粉彩的碗、盘、瓶、罐等。这些仿品由于是现代仿品，因此都具有共同的特点，有的胎体过于轻薄或过于厚重，所施色彩较薄或过厚，纹饰绘画过于精细、鲜亮，具有现代艺术品的气息。应引起我们注意的是器物款识。朝代款识仿得逼真，在鉴赏时必须结合造型、纹饰和色彩全面分析。但也有一些是仿制者编造的"某年某月"或较罕见的室名款。这些器物非常吸引收藏者，是格外要警惕的。

三　民国时期粉彩瓷器

辛亥革命推翻清王朝，建立中华民国后，为皇室专烧瓷器的御窑厂停办，全国瓷业进行改良，成立了不少瓷业公司，此时为了维持中国瓷业在国内外市场的需要，民国时涌现了大量的仿古瓷。上至六朝青瓷下到唐、五代、宋的名窑名品以及明清御窑中典型器几乎无不仿制，而且惟妙惟肖。时至今日，大量的民国仿品仍旧混迹人间，甚至也有不少流往海外。因此民国时期的仿品也是值得深入研究的问题。其中粉彩瓷器也是当时的生产主流。

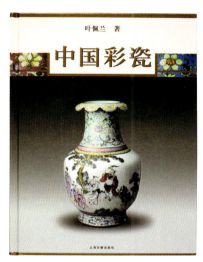

民国时期粉彩瓷器主要是以郭世五仿制的雍、乾粉彩、珐琅彩和带有斋堂款的粉彩最精美，其次是民间收藏的无款或书写清代各朝的伪款粉彩瓷以及所谓洪宪瓷等。

郭世五仿雍正、仿乾隆的粉彩珐琅彩最为精细，具有雍乾时彩瓷的风韵。据《景德镇史稿》、《明清瓷器鉴定》、《古玩旧闻》等著作介绍，袁世凯任大总统时曾派郭世五（原名郭葆昌）在景德镇担任陶务监督，是我国陶瓷史上最后一个督陶官。此人在担任督陶官前后的一段时间内，主要是发展仿古瓷。由于他常驻景德镇，对窑工熟悉，也有条件用重金聘用制瓷能手。郭氏仿雍正、乾隆的珐琅彩和粉彩瓷，胎质洁白，画工精细，色彩瑰丽。1949年郭氏亲属捐献给故宫博物院的瓷器中，就有多件郭氏珍品，以瓶为主，瓶体多为撇口灯笼式，器表纹饰主要以人物为主，有婴戏图、麻姑献寿图、高士图以及古代文人喜爱的琴、棋、书、画图案。继承乾隆时的施彩方法以料彩为主，部分纹饰施加粉彩，画面纹饰精美，生动活泼。其款识均为红彩篆书或楷书"居仁堂制"、"觯斋主人"、"陶务监督郭葆昌谨制"、"洪宪年制"、"洪宪御制"等。这种精品在当时古董界称为"洪宪"瓷或称民国珐琅彩。民国早期"洪宪"瓷已成为郭氏仿品的代称。由于制作水平高，当时"洪宪"瓷名噪一时，不少古董商因此牟取高利。

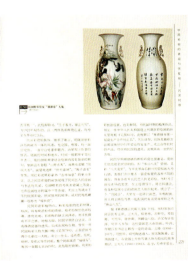

6. 民国粉彩仕女"福禄寿"大瓶：叶佩兰主编《中国彩瓷》，上海古籍出版社，2005年，第279页图799。

郭世五专为他自己烧制的仿雍正粉彩，也很精致，瓶高约达30厘米左右，绘盛开的花卉和草虫、蝴蝶，瓶底有两种款识，一种青花楷书"大清雍正年制"六字款，一种红彩篆书"郭世五"三字款。远效果鉴赏较为漂亮，具有一些雍正粉彩的韵味。仔细观赏足内面有较大的鬃眼，蓝色彩料偏黑灰调，彩料表面不光润，与雍正粉彩真品相比则相形见绌。

民国时期斋堂款的粉彩瓷器除郭世五的多种款识外，还有静远堂（为北洋军阀徐世昌专用品）、居仁堂（郭世五为袁世凯特制，具有清代御窑粉彩的风格，承德避暑山庄博物馆藏一件红彩篆书"居仁堂制"款的粉彩云蝠云龙纹赏瓶，通体纹饰加饰金彩边饰，显得金碧辉煌）。以上三个款识虽属民国器物，但在当时就有仿品，因同属一个年代，有时难以确认。

现在在民间仍传有"洪宪年制"或"洪宪御制"款的粉彩瓷器，多数均为当时的商品瓷。袁世凯称帝仅83天，袁倒台后一些古董商为招揽生意，将袁世凯未能正式运用的"洪宪"年号作为瓷器的款识，制作了许多"洪宪"款瓷器。绘画花卉、花鸟、人物纹饰。这些伪款的民间粉彩瓷风靡一时，国内外流传甚广。现在民间仍保留不少用青花或红彩写清代各朝伪款的粉彩餐具和茶具。以红彩楷书"乾隆年制"或图章式"乾隆年制"的伪款常见。还有"嫁妆瓷"应是民国时期的特殊产品。以大瓶、大盖罐为主，器体一面绘粉彩人物故事，一面是墨书诗句，有的还带干支纪年款及作者姓名，这类瓷器多为20世纪20年代前后的产品，有的画面也很生动，值得收藏。

当前文物市场上除仿明清各朝的官民窑瓷器外，其它各代瓷器都仿，连民国瓷器近些年也仿制很多。目前是陶瓷发展史上的第三次仿制高潮，第一次为雍正唐英任督陶官的仿制，第二次为民国时期的仿制。因此无论是收藏爱好者，还是博物馆工作者，都应该不断提高自己鉴别文物的水平，不然稍有不慎即难免失误。正如《论古瓷收藏误导》（《收藏》2000年2期）一文所言："不看懂真品，犹辨不清真伪. 不看懂伪品，也辨不清真伪。"这真是从实践中总结出来的道理。

The Appreciation of the Polychrome Porcelains of the Late Qing Dynasty to Minguo Era

Ye Peilan

In the past thousand years, the ancient ceramics of China displaying various styles in different times become our cultural treasures and enjoy great fame in the world.

In the early Qing Dynasty, especially the reigns of the first three emperors, the porcelain craftsmanship reached the climax, to the later period, because of the insufficient national strength, the court has ordered the official kiln to stop the production in the Jiaqing Era (1796-1820). However, the porcelain-making techniques of the official kiln were still preserved and developed, including the blue-and-white porcelains, the famille-rose porcelains and polychrome porcelains. For example, the light-crimson created in the Guangxu Era (1875-1908), the unique "official kiln famille-rose" created in Tongzhi and Guangxu Eras (1862-1908), the porcelain sculpture of Wang Bingrong and Chen Guozhi, the bisque porcelain of Li Zhiyuan and so on were all the new porcelain artwork types emerged in this time. The cloisonné enamel of the Minguo (Republic) Period imitating that of the Yongzheng (1723-1735) to Qianlong Eras (1736-1795) of the Qing Dynasty could also be listed together with them as the great breakthroughs of porcelain art over the past. Just as Chen Liu introduced in his *Taoya (Pottery Refinements)*, an encyclopedia on ceramics, that "in the early Qianlong Era, because it was not far from the Yongzheng Era, the entertainments and music and dancing were still very flourishing, as well as the handicrafts. After the middle Qianlong, they are not that skillful as that in Kangxi Era (1662-1722) and not that beautiful as that in Yongzheng Era, and just because of the not minding the costs, the porcelains could reach the middle level of that in the former two eras. Since the Jiaqing and Daoguang (1821-1850) Eras, both the coloring skills and the quality of the color materials have been getting worse and worse. However, the most elaborate artworks made in this period are still not to be neglected."

1, The Plate Painting of Mi Fu Bowing to the Rock, Minguo (1912-1949). Figure 57 of Zeng Meifang [ed]. 2003. *Jingdezhen Caici Sanbai Nian* (景德镇彩瓷三百年, *Jingdezhen Painted Porcelain in the Past 300 Years*). Nanchang: Jiangxi Fine Arts Publishing House.

(1) The Emergence of Light-crimson Porcelains

Light-crimson polychrome porcelain is a folk kiln product type with over-glaze colors prevailing in the late Qing Dynasty to early Minguo Period. The decorative designs of the light-crimson polychrome porcelain wares look like miniature traditional Chinese paintings. The colors of this kind of porcelain wares are pale and light, mainly light ocher, bluishness, aqua green, lawn green, accompanied by purple, red or other colors to form relaxing and gentle scenes. Because the light ocher is the most conspicuous color in this kind of porcelain, the term "Qianjiang" (浅绛, Light-crimson) of traditional Chinese painting art is borrowed to name it. Actually, light ocher may not be the most conspicuous color in every individual piece, the main tints of some artworks of this kind of porcelain are bluishness, light grey and so on. The paintings are imitating the gongbi (fine brushwork painting) style, therefore some scholars call this porcelain type as "multi-colored ink painting", which is also very insightful.

In fact, light-crimson is a polychrome porcelain type derived from the famille-rose porcelain. Its features different from those of famille-rose porcelain are that the color materials (or "pigments") contain more proportion of white color, the color layers are thinner, both of which make the colors lighter; because the body of the ware was not coated with "glass white" (mixed powder of lead oxide and silica) before coloring, and the colored surface was not covered with "snow-white glaze", the colors are dim and blurring with eroding and peeling off phenomena, which spoiled the beautiful appearance of the ware. The ground glaze of the light crimson ware is usually bluish-white glaze the thickness of which is sometimes uneven and seems wavy, the ones of which made in the Xuantong Era (1909-1911) and the early Minguo Period show lighter color.

The themes of the design of the light-crimson polychrome porcelain wares are mainly landscapes, human figures and tales, bird-and-flower design, antiquities and so on. According to the *Jingdezhen Jindai Taoren Lu (The Biographies of the Modern Ceramic Artists in Jingdezhen Kiln, by Liu Xinyuan)*, when doing the painting, the artists applied some skills of Wenrenhua (literati painting, one school of traditional Chinese painting art). The artisans decorating the light-crimson porcelains always had high cultural and artistic literacy, and were good at painting and calligraphy. They were also all-rounder on painting art: landscapes, human figures, bird-and-flower and fish-and-insect designs under their brushes are all vivid and true to life. From sketching to space arranging and from drawing to coloring and rendering of each artwork were all done by the same artisan. The motifs of the artworks are mostly adopted from the literati painting sketches, so their styles are looking more unrestrained and freehanded than that of the famille-rose products from the official kiln of Xuantong Era. Meanwhile, poems with contents related to the painting motifs, usually four-character, five-character or seven-character verses, are also written in the blank spaces of the artwork, followed by the date (represented by the way of stems-and-branches), place name where the work is done and the name of the artisan, showing the effect of the integration of poetry, calligraphy and painting arts in a porcelain ware. Light-crimson is a new specimen of polychrome porcelain in modern times.

3. The Vase with Elephant-Shaped Ears and Gold-traced Famille-rose Five-ethics (Five Birds Symbolizing Five Human Relations), Guangxu Era, Qing. Ibid. Figure 236.

The products of light-crimson porcelain were very popular in the society at the end of the 19th and the early 20th centuries. As the records of relevant literature, a group of celebrated light-crimson artists represented by Cheng Men and his eldest son named Cheng Yan, Jin Pinqing, Wang Youtang, Wang Shaowei, etc. are very influential at that time. The products circulated in the present-day markets show

that there were many masters of light-crimson porcelain around the end of the Qing Dynasty and the early Minguo Period, although names of most of them are lost. As the *Jingdezhen Shigao (A Draft History of Jingdezhen Kiln)*, since the beginning of the Minguo Period, the light-crimson porcelain technique vanished gradually.

The main categories of the light-crimson porcelain products are displaying porcelains and house wares. The displaying porcelains are plate paintings, vases in various shapes, such as the amphorae, cong-prism-tube shaped vases, mallet vases with lobed rims, square vases with flaring rims, and so on, and tubular hat racks in various shapes, such as cylindrical, square, cylindrical or hexagonal with openwork designs, which also had practical usages. Writing-brush pots of light-crimson products are all the small-sized circular ones appeared at the end of the Qing Dynasty. Tea utensils, lidded oblate mug, porridge jar, washer with flat rim and censer in various shapes are also popular types of light-crimson products. These daily utensils proved that light-crimson was a welcomed porcelain type in the common society.

Generally, the dates of making have been seen in the ink-written inscriptions of the paintings on the products; however, on the outer bottoms of the wares, the era name "Tongzhi" (同治) or "Tongzhi Nian Zhi" (同治年制, Made in Tongzhi Era), "Guangxu Nian Zhi" (光绪年制, Made in Guangxu Era) or the studio names of the artists are also written in seal script and red color, both of which are the typical features of polychrome porcelains produced by folk kilns in the late Qing Dynasty. In short, the light-crimson porcelain is an extraordinary invention in the history of Chinese ceramics during the late Qing Dynasty to the early Minguo Period.

(2) The Unique Famille-rose Porcelains of the Tongzhi, Guangxu and Xuantong Eras

The famille-rose porcelains collected in the Palace Museum are mostly tableware and displaying porcelains produced by the official kiln for the emperors and Empress

Dowager Cixi. According to the historic literature, for the imperial bridal in the seventh year of Tongzhi Era (1868), over 7000 pieces of porcelain wares were made under the supervision of Jingfu, the governor of Jiangxi Province. In Guangxu Era, tens of thousands of famille-rose porcelains with diversified ground colors were made for the birthday of Empress Dowager Cixi. The ground colors of these court-used porcelains, except for very few ones were cool colors, were dark or bright warm colors, such as scarlet, verdant, brilliant yellow or lavender, all of which are even and smooth, over which auspicious symbols of plentiful motifs are painted. The tableware assemblages for the imperial bridal used brilliant yellow as the ground color, over which golden "Shou" (寿, Longevity) character embraced by red bats (the name of which is metaphor of "happiness" in Chinese), five bats surrounding a "Shou" character, butterflies surrounding "Double-xi" (喜, happiness) character, plum blossoms and sparrows, bamboo grove and other more than a dozen of symbolic designs with auspicious connotations are painted, and all of these designs are permitted by the court. Today, we can still find the drafts of the porcelain design motifs in the Palace Museum Library.

5, The Imitation Cloisonné Enamel "Holy Hermit", Minguo Period [with Detail of "Made Solemnly by Guo Baochang, the Ceramic Supervisor" Inscription]. Figure 59 of Ye Peilan. 2005. *Gu Ci Bianshi* (古瓷辨识, *Appraising Ancient Chinese Ceramics*). Jinan: Shandong Fine Arts Publishing House.

In the Tongzhi Era, the famille-rose porcelains with white ground color have light designs, the motifs of which are usually plucked flowers and plants. At this time, the "medallion" design on colored grounds popular in Qianlong and Jiaqing Eras has almost disappeared, only on the famille-rose porcelains made for the imperial bridal, medallion designs with dragon and phoenix motifs could be seen. The famille-rose porcelains with white ground color made in Guangxu Era could be classified into the fine ones and rough ones. The fine ones are as exquisite as the ones made in Daoguang Era, the bird and flower designs of which are vivid and the colors are brilliant; on the bottoms, the date signature "Da Qing Guangxu Nian Zhi" (大清光绪

年制, Made in Guangxu Era of Great Qing) in regular script is seen. The rough ones are plates, bowls and washers with flat rims in large sizes, the bodies of which are thick and heavy, the colors are dark, dense and thick, and the designs, which are mainly dragon and phoenix or flowers, are bold and sketchy. In this period, the imitations of the large famille-rose "Nine-peach" vases and the famille-rose "One Hundred-deer" zun-jars in Qianlong style are very popular, but the imitations are often with thick and coarse bodies and gaudy colors, and the designs are stiff without three-dimensional effect.

Some special samples of famille-rose porcelains are found in Tongzhi and Guangxu Eras, such as: 1, The famille-rose ash trough of Tongzhi Era [Figure 705 in *Zhongguo Caici* (中国彩瓷, *Chinese Decorative Porcelain*)], the body of which is like a rectangular washer, one side of which is erecting out of the rim as a cloud-shaped back. The back and the other three sides of the trough are decorated with famille-rose butterflies, flowers, plants and other insects, which is the motif of "having passed the palace examination as the third highest grade". This is said to be set in front of the brazier or fireplace as the ash container. 2, The famille-rose three-fruit round case with yellow ground color. On the lid of the case, a citron, a pomegranate and a peach are carved in high relief surrounding a flying bat, the metaphor of which is "fortune and three plenty – happiness, longevity and high status". On the outer bottom, the signature "Wang Bingrong" is engraved, which is the name of a famous porcelain sculptor. This kind of famille-rose porcelain sculpture is peculiar to the Tongzhi Era. 3, The "Awarding Vase". It is a famille-rose porcelain type made for the court to award to the officials or to display popular since the Qianlong Era. The typical shape of the awarding vase is flaring rim, long neck, a ring of bowstring pattern is applied on the shoulder, round belly, and the date is written on the outer bottom in red or blue color.

The vases of this shape are cataloged as "Yutangchun" vase in the court archives of the Qing Dynasty. In the late Qing Dynasty, the shapes of awarding vases became diversified, such as the prism-tube-shaped vase with Eight-trigram pattern and the glaze of Ge Kiln style, ovoid vase with tube-shaped lugs and flambé glaze, paper pulp-mallet vase with "Chang Guan" (official kiln) glaze (or tea-dust glaze) and so on. In the Guangxu Era, flask-shaped vase with straight neck and blue-and-white cloud and bat design appeared as a peculiar type. 4, Floor Vase, Large Jar and Large Flower Pot. These large-sized famille-rose porcelain wares are elegantly shaped and exquisitely decorated, the peony motif of which is the most outstanding example, and the colors are brilliantly applied. The floor vases made in Guangxu Era are as large as 130-150 cm high, the large flower pots, 50 cm high and 40-50 cm in diameter. It is not difficult to recognize that the technique of burning large-sized porcelain wares in the late Qing Dynasty was still very high. 5, The famille-rose porcelain wares with "Da Ya Zhai" (大雅斋, Great Elegance Studio) inscription, which are peculiar to the Guangxu Era. The main categories are plate, bowl, case, high-foot dish, high-foot bowl, spoon, bowl-shaped mug, round case, flower pot, large jar and so on. The decoration themes are bird-and-flower, the main motifs of which are birds and wisteria, birds and grape, herons and lotus flowers, and so on, usually very innovative. The "Da Ya Zhai" inscription is generally written horizontally from right to left in red color, beside which is the oval seal with five characters "Tian Di Yi Jia Chun" (天地一家春), which was the name of a mansion in Yuanming Yuan (Old Summer Palace) where Empress Dowager Cixi has lived when she was an imperial concubine. This type of two inscriptions (signatures) marked on a single ware is also peculiar to the Guangxu Era. 6, The "Autumn Maneuver Souvenir" Cup. During the Guangxu Era, several times of military maneuvers have been conducted in the

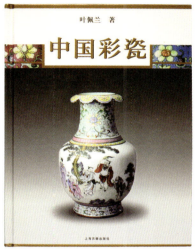

6, The Large Vase with Famille-rose Beauty Figure and Happiness-Fortune-Longevity Design (Deer, Bats and Cranes), Minguo Period. Figure 799 of Ye Peilan. 2005. *Zhongguo Caici* (中国彩瓷, *Chinese Decorative Porcelain*). Shanghai Shanghai Chinese Classics Publishing House.

autumns, and the cups are made as souvenirs for them. The most popular three types of this kind of cups are: the pink peony-shaped ones and the green-lotus-leaf-shaped ones, both of which have handles made as pedicel or stalk, and the handles are hollow and linked to the inside of the cups, so they are also called "sucking cups". On the back of the handles, the date and location of the maneuver for which the cup is made are written in dark color. The third type is in the shape of common wine cup, the outer wall of which is decorated with cloud-and-dragon design and the date and location of the maneuver are written below the rim.

The inscriptions on different famille-rose porcelain products of the official kiln in the late Qing Dynasty have different contents and styles. Generally, only the date of making is written on the outer bottom of the ware in under-glaze blue and regular script. The utensils made for the imperial bridal of Emperor Tongzhi are marked "Tongzhi Nian Zhi" (同治年制, made in Tongzhi Era), "Chang Chun Tong Qing" (长春同庆, Congratulating the Ever-lasting) or "Yan Xi Tong He" (燕喜同和, Happy Bridal and Perfect Match) and other four-character greeting words. The displaying porcelains made in Guangxu Era have the inscription "Yong Qing Chang Chun" (永庆长春, Celebrating Forever the Ever-lasting), or the names of the halls and palaces such as "Le Shou Tang" (乐寿堂), "Ti He Dian" (体和殿), "Chang Chun Gong" (长春宫) and so on. As mentioned above, the utensils specially made for Empress Dowager Cixi have the combination of "Da Ya Zhai" (大雅斋) and "Tian Di Yi Jia Chun" (天地一家春) as their unique inscriptions.

The Famille-rose Porcelain Products of the Xuantong Era. Xuantong Era lasted for only three years, during which the official kiln in Jingdezhen was still burning famille-rose porcelains for the court, but, seen from the ones in present-day collections, these products are all the replicas of those types appeared in Guangxu Era, the difference between which is only the date marked on their bottoms. The only one product of this period could be appreciated is the famille-rose Yuhuchun vase (pear-shaped vase) with peony motif, which has the taste of Yongzheng famille-rose porcelains, the suitable tints and exquisite decorations with perspective effect and could be regarded as a masterpiece of the official kiln in the late Qing Dynasty. In Hanhai Auction, the hammer price for one piece of this kind of product was over 200,000 CNY, showing that it wins strong favor from the collectors.

The modern imitations of the famille-rose porcelains of the Jiaqing and thereafter eras of the Qing Dynasty can be often seen today, most of which are that of the popular ones or the famous ones of the official kiln, such as the famille-rose porcelains with color grounds and Jiaqing date inscription, the ones with Daoguang date and Shende Tang (慎德堂) maker inscriptions, the bowls, plates, vases and jars with Tongzhi, Guangxu and Xuantong date inscriptions, etc. Because these imitations bearing different date inscriptions are actually modern products made within close dates, they share many common features: the bodies are usually too thin and light or too thick and heavy, the colors are too light or too dark, and the decorations are too fine, elaborate and brilliant, reflecting the spirit of modern artworks. What we must pay much attention to is the inscriptions, which is the easiest to be imitated true to life. When we identify them, we must consider them together with the shaping, decorative design and colors as a whole. However, some forgers may fabricate some rare or even never-seen-before date or studio inscriptions. The wares with these rare inscriptions are very attractive to the collectors and therefore we should especially guard against this kind of forgeries.

(3) The Famille-rose Porcelains of the Minguo Period

Since the Xinhai Revolution overthrowing the Qing Dynasty and Founding the Republic of China (Minguo), the official kiln producing porcelains for the imperial court was closed down. The porcelain industry in the whole country was reorganized and many porcelain companies were established. To meet the demands in both domestic and abroad markets, large amounts of imitation antique porcelains emerged in the Minguo Period. The imitations from the celadon wares of the Six Dynasties via the celebrated products of the famous kilns of the Tang, the Five-Dynasties and the Song Dynasty to the typical products of the official kilns of the Ming and Qing Dynasties were all made vividly and could hardly be told from the original ones. Even at present, many imitation antique porcelain wares made in the Minguo Period are still hidden or circulated in and among private collections and even exported abroad. So, the antique porcelain imitation of the Minguo Period is also a topic waiting for in-depth research. Among these imitations, famille-rose is also a mainstream.

The best famille-rose porcelains in the Minguo Period are the ones imitating the famille-rose and enamel polychrome porcelains of the Yongzheng and Qianlong Eras of the Qing Dynasty and the famille-rose ones with certain "Zhai" (斋) or "Tang" (堂, studio or hall) inscriptions, all of which are made under the supervision of Guo Shiwu. Following them, the famille-rose porcelains with faked date inscriptions or without any inscriptions are also popular, most of which are in private collections. The so-called Hongxian (the era title of Yuan Shikai when he was enthroned by himself) Porcelain are also good cases of famille-rose wares.

The famille-rose and enamel polychrome porcelains made under Guo Shiwu's supervision. They have the artistic styles and tastes of the Yongzheng and Qianlong Eras of the Qing Dynasty. According to the *Jingdezhen Shigao (A Draft History of Jingdezhen Kiln)*, *Ming Qing Ciqi Jianding (The Identification of the Ming and Qing Porcelains)* and *Guwan Tan Jiuwen (Anecdotes on the Antique Collecting)* and other relevant works, when Yuan Shikai was on the position of the president, he assigned Guo Shiwu (whose old name was Guo Baochang) as the ceramic supervisor in Jingdezhen Kiln, which was the final ceramic supervisor in the history of Chinese ceramics. On his post, Guo paid his efforts mainly to the making of imitation antique porcelains. Because he was familiar with Jingdezhen and the potters, he had condition to hire able masters with suitable salaries. The famille-rose and enamel polychrome porcelains made under his supervision have fine and clean bodies, exquisite decorative designs and luxurious colors. Among the porcelains donated by Guo Shiwu's relatives to the Palace Museum, there were many masterpieces made under his supervision, most of which were vases in the shape of lantern with flaring rim. The motifs of these porcelains are mainly human figures, such as playing children, "Magu Presenting Longevity", "Holy Hermits" and the scenes of playing zither, chess, reading book and appreciating paintings, which are the favorite motifs of ancient literati class. The coloring technique was also succeeded from that of the Qianlong Era, which was mainly the glass colors accompanied with famille-rose colors in details. The designs are painted finely and elaborately and the scenes are depicted vividly and animatedly. Their inscriptions are "Juren Tang Zhi" (居仁堂制, Made in Juren Hall), "Zhi Zhai Zhuren" (觯斋主人, the Host of Zhi Studio), "Taowu Jiandu Guo Baochang Jin Zhi" (陶务监督郭葆昌谨制, Made Solemnly by Guo Baochang, the Ceramic Supervisor), "Hongxian Nian Zhi" (洪宪年制, Made in Hongxian Era), "Hongxian Yu Zhi" (洪宪御制, Made for Imperial Use of Hongxian) and so on. These masterpieces were known as "Hongxian Porcelains" or "Minguo Enamel Wares" in the antique collecting circle at that time. In the early Minguo Period, "Hongxian Porcelain" has become the exclusive term referring to the imitation antique porcelains made under Guo's supervision. Because the high imitating level, the Hongxian Porcelains enjoyed sudden fame at that time and because of which many antique dealers earned huge profits.

The imitation famille-rose porcelains of the Yongzheng Era made by Guo Shiwu for himself are also very skillful: the vases are about 30 cm in height, on which blossoming flowers, plants and flying butterflies and other insects are painted. On the bottoms of these wares, two kinds of inscriptions are marked: one is "Da Qing Yongzheng Nian Zhi" (大清雍正年制, Made in Yongzheng Era of Great Qing) written in regular script and blue color, the other is "Guo Shiwu" written in seal script and red color. The full-views of these products are rather graceful with tastes of Yongzheng famille-rose. However, if they are closely observed, the hair holes can be seen, the blue color shows dark grey hue and all of the colors are not smooth and sleek, which all cannot get up with the genuine

Yongzheng famille-rose wares.

In addition to the ones with Guo Shiwu's inscriptions, the famille-rose porcelains made in Minguo Period also the pieces with inscription of "Jingyuan Tang" (静远堂, The Hall of Quietude and Foresight), which are made for Xu Shichang, one of the Beiyang Warlords, and the ones with "Juren Tang" (居仁堂, Hall of Benevolence), which are made for Yuan Shikai with the styles of official kiln famille-rose products of the Qing Dynasty (the typical sample is an awarding vase with cloud-and-dragon and bat designs and golden rim collected in Museum of Mountain Hamlet for Escaping Heat, Chengde). The famille-rose products with these three kinds of inscriptions are all made in the Minguo Era, but because their imitations are made contemporaneously with them, so they are usually hard to identify.

The famille-rose porcelains bearing "Hongxian Nian Zhi" (洪宪年制), or "Hongxian Yu Zhi" (洪宪御制), are actually commercial products made on orders of the antique dealers. Yuan Shikai was enthroned as "emperor" by himself for only 83 days. After his collapse, these antique dealers used "Hongxian" (洪宪), the era title drafted by Yuan Shikai but not formally proclaimed, as the date inscriptions on the porcelains including famille-rose products to attract customers. The famille-rose porcelains with "Hongxian" inscriptions are mostly decorated with bird-and-flower and human figure motifs. These famille-rose porcelains made by folk kilns with forged inscriptions were popular both at home and abroad, even at present, lots of famille-rose porcelain tableware and tea ware bearing date inscriptions of the eras of the Qing Dynasty written in blue or red colors are still found in private collections, mostly those with Qianlong marks in regular script or stamp format. The so-called "dowry porcelain" would be the famille-rose products peculiar to the Minguo Period. The main types of this kind of products are large vases and large lidded jars, one side of which is painted with human figures or story scenes, the other side is ink-written poems, sometimes accompanied with dates in stems-and-branches format and the name of the artist making this piece or the author of the poem. These famille-rose porcelains are mostly the products around 1920s, some of which are made exquisitely with vivid designs and worthy of collecting.

In addition to that of the products of the official and folk kilns of the Ming and Qing Dynasties, the imitations of the porcelains of other periods, including that of the Minguo Period, are frequently seen in the cultural relics markets today. At present, the third wave of antique porcelain imitating is taking place: the first wave is the imitating movement conducted by Tang Ying, the ceramic-producing supervisor in the Yongzheng Era of the Qing Dynasty and the second one is the imitating in the Minguo Period. So, both the amateur collectors and the professional museum curators need to raise the skill of identifying antiques, otherwise, it will be unavoidable to make mistakes. Just as the paper titled *Lun Guci Shoucang Wudao* (论古瓷收藏误导, *On the Misleading in the Antique Porcelain Collections*) in *Shoucang* (收藏, *Collections*) No. 2, 2000 says, "If you do not understand the genuine antiques, you cannot tell them from the forgeries. If you do not understand the forgeries, you still cannot tell them from the genuine antiques." This is really the truth drawn from the practices.

"双轨制"文物艺术品鉴定方法在规避文物艺术品投资风险中的作用

张崇檀

　　文物艺术品投资的风险产生于对器物本身真伪、品相的判断，以及对其价值、价值增长空间的判断之中，风险规避即要甄别器物，对其市场行情作出正确的预判。以投资为目的的器物鉴定，是在保真的前提下准确判断其在一定时期内的价值增长空间。眼学鉴定与科技鉴定的结合，有效避免单一鉴定方式的弊端，能够对器物的历史时期、历史背景进行正确的甄别，并对其收藏现状、市场表现予以精准的判断，从而达到规避文物艺术品投资的风险的目的。

　　一　投资风险的存在及其特征

　　以文物艺术品为标的的投资建立在文物艺术品的历史属性和文化属性的基础上，并直接诉求于文物艺术品在一定时间段内的价值增长空间。文物艺术品投资在形态上不同于传统的文物艺术品收藏，它在一定时期内以购入和售出为手段，实现文物艺术品的潜在价值空间，从而达到资本增长的目的，而文物艺术品的收藏是以对文物艺术品的所有权的占有为依据，它诉求于文物艺术品的价值本身，并且不以价值的实现为目的。

　　自上世纪八九十年代国内收藏市场兴起以来，文物艺术品的收藏就面临了甄别与鉴定的问题。文物艺术品收藏的风险来自对器物本身的认识错误，即对器物的历史时期、背景资料、存世情况、市场行情的认识出现偏差，或将仿制的器物误判为真品，从而导致高价购入的状况发生，并且在收藏市场还不成熟的情况下，仿制现象也颇普遍，一些仿品几可乱真，收藏市场上也存在人为的炒作，以及对市场的误导，这就人为增加了甄别的难度，使收藏风险大为增加。

　　以收藏为目的的文物艺术品鉴定，集中在器物"是什么"这个方面，风险也来自对器物"是什么"的认识出现的偏差。文物艺术品的收藏中风险的规避，建立在对文物艺术品本身的价值的正确判断的基础上，因此，它是以保真为规避方式的。"保真"即对器物本身"是什么"给出正确的判断，以此作为收藏的依据。

　　文物艺术品投资是市场发展到一定程度后出现的现象，它是资本运作在文物艺术品市场上的体现。文物艺术品投资的先决条件是文物艺术品的收藏，它在形式上表现为藏品的转让。为实现投资的目的，投资者需要以低价购入，并以高价售出。文物艺术品的价值依据是文物艺术品的社会稀缺程度与藏家的收藏欲望的迫切程度的对比关系，它涉及器物本身，以及器物的市场表现。文物艺术品属于历史存留，它的供给基本上不会发生变动，在收藏界对器物的认识没有发生改变的情况下，器物的市场价值不会产生大的波动，而只遵循收藏市场的一般价值规律。这种情况下，文物艺术品是不具备投资价值的，它的价格上涨幅度有限，并且存在下跌的风险。具有投资价值的文物艺术品，必然存在一个潜在的价值空间，这个价值空间来自收藏市场上的认识偏差，即收藏市场低估了器物的珍贵程度。

因此，文物艺术品投资的风险，不仅存在于对器物本身甄别的正确与否上，更存在于对其价值增长空间的把握程度上。投资者要在保真的基础上对器物的价值增长空间作出判断，预见到一定时期内收藏市场会对该器物的价值重新估量，或者具有引导市场对该器物的价值进行重新估量的能力。当收藏市场对该器物的价值有了新的判断之后，文物艺术品的价值增长空间才有了实现的可能，并且这个可能还要以器物转让的实际发生为标志。

文物艺术品投资的风险，更多的表现在高价售出的实现上，即投资者不能按照预期的时间和价格成功售出以投资为目的购入的文物艺术品。文物艺术品投资不同于文物艺术品的收藏，它是资本运作在艺术品收藏领域的体现，它追求的是一定时间内的资金回报率，而不是对文物艺术品及其价值的实际占有。因此，只有当以投资为目的购入的文物艺术品按照预期的时间与价格成功售出，文物艺术品投资的风险才算完全规避。

二　风险规避的应有条件

文物艺术品投资的风险存在于三个方面，一是对器物本身的甄别，一是对器物价值增长空间的把握，一是器物预期售出的成功与否。因此，在文物艺术品的投资中进行风险规避，一是要对作为投资标的的器物进行正确的甄别，一是要对器物的市场表现情况进行准确的预判，一是对该器物在预期的时间段内市场上收藏欲望和收藏群体有清晰的把握，能够及时实现藏品到资本的转换。

三　"双轨制"文物艺术品鉴定方法的具体实施

"双轨制"文物艺术品鉴定方法是传统的眼学鉴定与现代的科技鉴定的结合，这个结合既是技术文明的进步在文物艺术品领域内的反映，又是文物艺术品行业自身发展的必然结果。按照正常的学术发展规律，当一个稳定的学术体系内部存在的缺陷日益凸显，新的学术观点和学术体系就会在弥补这个缺陷的基础上产生。"双轨制"正是在文物艺术品的行业经营由传统的收藏向投资转向的条件下提出的，它所要解决的是文物艺术品投资中存在的风险问题。

传统的眼学鉴定是基于标型的鉴定方法，它以古墓葬出土的同类器物或传世的可信器物为标准器，并与可信的文献互相印证，以材质、颜色、造型、纹饰、款识等为依据，通过与标准器的对比大致确定器物的时代和背景。标型学的前提在于标准器的认定，以及鉴定者对标准器具有的识别信息的理解程度，这是以个人经验或行业共识为依据的，这个经验包括鉴真的经验和辨伪的经验，其中辨伪的经验主要是指对仿制器物、相似器物的识别。考古痕迹学也属于眼学鉴定的范围，它是通过事件发生后的内在或外在的痕迹，推论出导致这些痕迹发生的原因或过程，以此为依据对器物的背景情况有一个大致的判断。在解决器物的真伪之后，眼学鉴定还要辨别器物的存世情况和收藏情况，对该器物的收藏行情有一个正确的认识，并能为具体的器物估出一个大致的经济价值范围。即眼学鉴定既要解决器物"是什么"的问题，又要解决"怎么样"的问题，为收藏、投资提供依据。藏家把器物拿来做鉴定，通常包含了对器物本身的真伪的要求和器物的市场行情的要求。

眼学鉴定的专家大致可以分为几个类型，即文博系统专家、考古系统专家、文物经营专家，以及收藏经验丰富的藏家等。不同类型的专家有着不同的知识体系和文化背景，对器物的鉴别也有着不同的思路，把他们的鉴定思路、鉴别依据、甄别结果综合考量和互相印证，能够得到一个可以信赖的鉴定结果，这个鉴定结果是能够被目前的收藏界信服的。但是因为眼学鉴定中人为因素的大量存在，以及鉴定资质的认定缺少依据，藏家也没有可行的方法对鉴定结果进行确认。

对这个已有的文物艺术品鉴定的学术体系的补救，首先要解决证真和证伪的问题。眼学鉴定是建立在一定学术背景下的论证和推断，鉴定结果的完整表述应该是"根据现有资料进行推测，该器物应该是某器物"，这些观点是不能证真或证伪的。新的方法的提出，应该在传统的眼学鉴定的经验主义的基础上给出事实的论证，而科技鉴定的可信数据，是对器物身份问题的有力证明。

科技鉴定是用仪器检测为手段的鉴定方法，从类型上分为年代检测、成分检测和结构检测等。年代检测利用一定的物理原理或化学原理对检测到的数据进行分析或对比，主要方法有碳十四、热释光、加速器质谱仪、电子自旋共振、热剩磁等，它建立在器物的测量数据不受干扰的前提下，即检测之前没有外在因素致使器物的待检指标发生改变。成分分析法有两种类型，一是微量取样，用化学方法或物理方法进行成分分析，一是用各种粒子(电子、中子、质子等)激发受测样本，使其发出X射线能谱，从谱线分析各元素的含量。结构分析包括宏观结构和微观结构，即对不同成分的组合方式的分析，以及对分子结构、原子结构的分析。成分分析、结构分析仍然建立在"标型"的理论基础上，成分分析和结构分析是对器物的物质构成进行的分析，这个分析的结果本身是没有意义的，而必须要和标准器的物质构成分析的数据库结合起来，从而判断检测器物在物质构成上与标准器是否一致。

科技鉴定在解决现存问题的同时，也先天带有一些弊端，这是由具体鉴定方法的各自原理和实施方法决定的。科技鉴定建立在器物的物质构成的物理属性或化学属性的基础上，它测量的仅仅是该器物的物质构成的物理属性或化学属性，并且这个测量结果存在一个允许的误差范围。对科技鉴定的补救，是将科技检测的结果作为参考依据，综合纳入眼学鉴定的论证中去，而不仅仅以测量得到的数据与标准器的数据一致作为判定依据。眼学鉴定的经验对测量结果也有一定的修正作用，鉴定者能够根据对器物的了解，调整科技鉴定的误差。

双轨制的实施，是将传统的眼学鉴定与新兴的科技鉴定融为一体，对器物的身份问题进行合理的推断。断定一件器物为真，原则上要求任何一种鉴定方式得到的结果都不存在可疑之处，即目前的条件下对该器物为真不存在存疑之处。而断定一件器物非真，只需要找到一处存疑的地方，即对该器物为真存在反对的理由。这种双轨的鉴定方式，是在现有的学术背景下应该持有的一个严谨态度。双轨制判定为真的，现有的鉴定方式都支持器物为真，已经排除了存疑，目前的学术界和收藏界提不出反对其为真的依据。这种情况下，器物的价值本身是可以确定的，它的价值增长空间也可以因此确定。双轨制判定为非真的，是因为鉴定得到的结果存在可疑之处，这是一种谨慎的态度，它并不排除器物为真的可能性，但从投资角度来说，它对可能存在的风险进行了最有效的规避。

双轨制的实施，是眼学鉴定与科技鉴定的结合，这个结合是就方法上而言的，而不是就专家而言的。它是各个鉴定方法的结合，即利用现有的鉴定方法，对器物分别鉴定，再进行互相印证，尽可能排除人为因素的干扰，从而得到一个论证过的综合意见。这样的一个鉴定结果，是文物艺术品投资中能够成功规避风险的基础和保证。

文物艺术品投资中对文物艺术品的价值增长空间的判定和对预期市场行情的判定，是通过眼学鉴定实现的。双轨制是鉴定方法上的双轨，其中眼学鉴定部分既包括了标型学、痕迹学的鉴定，还包括市场行情的判断。文博系统专家、考古系统专家、文物经营专家、科技鉴定专家，以及收藏经验丰富的藏家等都属于双轨制的鉴定系统，针对具体的文物艺术品进行投资时，双轨制会将他们各自的意见汇集起来进行综合的论证。这个论证的结果包含了对器物真伪的说明，以及对其市场行情、价值增长的判断，以及可能存在的风险。以此为依据进行文物艺术品的投资，是在现有的条件下进行风险规避的合理方式。

The Function of "Dual System" of Antique Authentication in the Risk Averse of Art Investment

Zhang Chongtan

The risk of art investment happens in the estimations to the genuineness and perfectness of the artworks and the judgments to their values and increasing potentials. The risk averse of art investment refers to the correct authentication of the artworks and the accurate predict to their future markets. The task of antique authentication aiming on investment is to accurately estimate the value increasing potential of an antique artwork in a given period in the premise that it has been confirmed to be genuine. The association of traditional visual verification and modern scientific identification may avoid the weakness of single identification method, correctly determine the date and historic background of an antique artwork and accurately estimate its collection situation and market appearance, in order to avert the risk of antique art investment.

(1) The Existence of Invest Risk and its Characteristics

The art investment with antique artworks as object is based on the historic and cultural attributions of the antique artworks and in pursuit of the value increasing potential of these artworks in a given period. The antique art investment differs from the traditional antique artwork collecting in terms of meanings: it materializes the value increasing potentials of the antique artworks by purchasing and selling them at a time difference. On the contrary, antique artwork collecting is aiming on the possession of the antique artworks themselves. It pursues the artistic values of the antique artworks rather than the materialization of their financial values.

Since the flourishing of the art market in mainland China in the 1980s, the collecting of antique artworks has been facing the problems of authentication and identification. The risk of antique artwork collecting comes from the wrong understanding to the natures of the antiques, including their historic periods, backgrounds, provenances and marketing statuses, or the misjudging of fakes as genuine antiques, all of which can result in overestimation of the values of the objects and purchasing with unreasonably high prices. Meanwhile, in the yet immature art market, imitations are very popular, some of which almost cannot be distinguished from the genuine antiques, the intentional malicious boasting and misleading also exist in the art market. All of these make the authentication and identification more difficult and raise the risk of antique artwork collecting cause.

The identification of artworks for the purpose of collection, focuses on the aspect of "what this artwork is", while the risk also comes from the aberrations of the knowledge on "what it is". The risk aversion of art collection is based on the correct determination to the cultural value of the artwork itself, therefore, the way of risk aversion is "guaranteeing the genuineness", which is accurately judging "what this artwork is", which is used as the basis of collection.

Antique art investment is a phenomenon occurring at the time when the antique art market developed to a certain extent, and it is the embodiment of the capital operation in the art market. The prerequisite for investment in antique art collection is manifested in the form of the transfer of collections. To achieve the purpose of investment, investors need to buy at low and sell at high prices. The value estimation of an antique artwork is based on the relativity of the rareness of this antique artwork in the society and the urgency of the desire of collectors to collect it, which involves the artwork itself as well as its market performance. Antique artwork is handed down from the history, its supply usually does not change, when the collection industry's understanding to it does not change, its market value will not produce large fluctuations, but only to follow the general market value of the antique art collection. In this case, antique artwork does not have the investment value: its price rises are limited, and there are downside risks. The antique artworks with investment value are bound to an increasing potential space, which comes from the misunderstanding in the antique art market, that is, the market underestimated the preciousness of the object.

Therefore, the antique art investment risk exists not only in the identification of the artworks themselves, but also in the grasping of the growth space of their values. Based on the guaranteed genuineness, the investors should be able to judge the value increasing potential of the antique artwork and foresee that the art market will reassess its value in a short future, or to actively guide the art market to reassess its value. Only if the art market has new estimation to the value of an antique artwork, this artwork could possibly fulfill its value increasing, but this increasing still needs to be materialized by the actual transfer of the object.

Risks of antique art investment are more performed in the realization of selling at higher prices, which is that whether the investors can successfully sell the antique artworks bought in for the purpose of investment at the time and price as expected. Different from the antique art collection, antique art investment is the embodiment of capital operation in the field of art collection. It is the pursuit of money within a certain time for the investment return rate, rather than the actual possession of the artworks and their cultural and historic values. Therefore, only when the purchased artworks for investment purposes are sold with the expected time and the price, the risk of investment could be considered to be completely averted.

(2) The Prerequisites of Risk Averse of Art Investment

Antique art investment risk exists in three aspects, namely the authenticating of the artifacts themselves, the grasping of the value increasing potential of the artifacts, and the success of the selling of them. Therefore, to avoid the risk in the antique art investment, an investor should be able to correctly identify the objects first, accurately predict the market performance of the objects, and clearly understand the collecting desire and collector group of the objects in the antique art market so as to timely achieve the conversion from the artworks to the capital.

(3) The Concrete Conducting of the "Dual System" of Antique Artwork Authentication

"Dual system" of antique artwork authentication is the integration of traditional visual verification with naked eyes (or under the help of optical instruments) and scientific identification method with modern technologies, which is both the reflection of the technological advances in the field of antique art collection and the inevitable result of the development of the art collection industry itself. According to the rules of normal academic development, when defects within a stable academic system have become increasingly prominent, the new academic points of view and the academic systems will emerge on the basis of compensating for these defects. "Dual system" is put forward on the moment for the antique artwork collection industry to turn from the traditional possession to the investment, the problems for which it must solve is the risk existing in the antique art investment.

The traditional visual verification is based on typological identification methods, which uses the archaeologically unearthed artifacts with exact dates or clear stratigraphical relations, or objects handed down with reliable provenances as standard artifacts, and cross-checks with the credible literature, based on the material, color, shape, decoration, inscription and other features of the being identified objects compared with those of standard artifacts to roughly determine the age and background of these objects. The premise of typology is the definition of standard artifacts, and the levels of the appraisers' understandings to the identifiable information bore by these standard artifacts, which is based on personal experience and/or trade consensus. This experience includes the confirmation of the genuine antiques and the detection of forgeries, which mainly refers to the imitation objects or the objects similar to the genuine ones. Archaeological trace studies also belong to the visual verification, which is, based on the internal or external traces after the incident, to infer the reasons and process leading to the occurrence of these traces, as a basis for a general judgment to the background of the objects. In addressing the authenticity of objects, the visual verification also needs to make clear the collection desire and extant quantity in collection so as to have a correct understanding to the market of the objects and to provide a rough estimation of the economic value range to the specific objects. The visual verification should solve not only the issue of "what the object is" , but also the issue of "how the object is going to be" to provide the basis for the collection and investment. The collectors asking for authentication of the objects usually hope to solve the problem of authenticity of the artifacts themselves as well as the of market requirements and market demands to their collections.

The experts of visual verification can be sorted into several types, namely the experts in the cultural relics and museology fields, the experts of archeology, the experts on antique artwork management, and experienced connoisseurs and collectors. The experts of different types have different knowledge systems and cultural backgrounds. The comprehensive consideration and cross-proofing of their identifying ideas, reasons and results can draw a reliable authentication conclusion which is acceptable in the current art collection field. However, because the large amounts of human factors are involved in the visual verification, and the qualification of these experts are hardly authorized, the collectors have no feasible way to confirm the results of the authentication.

The compensation for the existing identification system must first solve the problems of authentication and falsification. The visual verification is the reasoning and inference built on a certain academic context, the full expression of the identification results of which should be "based on available information to speculate that this artifact should be a certain artifact", but this result can be neither authenticated nor falsified. The proposing of a new method should provide the reliable conclusion to the traditional visual verification on the empirical basis. However, the credible data obtained through scientific verification will be the powerful confirmation to the identity of the tested object.

Scientific verification is authentication method using means of instrument detection, which can be classified as chronological detection, composition detection and structure detection. Chronological detection applies certain principles of physics or chemistry to analyze or compare the data obtained in the detection, the main methods of which are radiocarbon dating, TL (Thermoluminescence), AMS (accelerator mass spectrometry), electron spin resonance, thermal remanence, etc. It is based on the premise that the testing data of the artifacts measurements are not interfered with, or that no external factors before testing resulted in the changes of the indicators of the objects to be tested. Component analysis has two types, one of which is micro-sampling, that is using chemical or physical methods for composition analysis, the other is to use a variety of particles (electrons, neutrons, protons, etc.) to stimulate the tested sample to emit X-ray spectroscopy, and then to do spectral analysis of elements from the content. Structural analysis, including macro-structural analysis and micro-structural analysis, is the analysis to the combination patterns of different components, as well as molecular structure, atomic structure analysis. Composition analysis and structural analysis are still based on the "typology" theory. They are the analyses to the material composition of the objects, the result of which is meaningless in itself. Only when the result is compared with its counterparts in the analysis result database of the standard artifacts, this material composition of the object under test could be determined that if it is consistent with that of the standard artifacts.

While solving the existing problems, the scientific verification also has some inherent drawbacks, which is defined by a specific method of implementation of their principles and methods of conduction. Scientific verification is built on the basis of the identification of the physical or chemical properties of the materials of the object under testing, its measurements are only to the physical and chemical properties of the material composition of the objects, and these measurements have a permissible error range. The compensation of the scientific verification is to use the test results as a reference comprehensively integrated into the reasoning process of the visual verification, rather than to simply use the comparison of the data with that of the standard artifact as a device to determine the identity of the object. Visual verification based on the experiences can also calibrate the measurement results, and the appraisers can adjust the errors in the scientific verification based on the understanding to the objects.

The implementation of "Dual System" is the integration of the traditional visual identification and the new-emerging scientific identification technologies, which can reasonably estimate the identity of the objects. In principle, to determine an object as genuine, it is required that the results got in all of the identifying methods are not suspicious, that is, the objects under the current conditions are no doubt to be genuine. On the contrary, to conclude an object as a fake, what should be done is only to find a place to doubt to be genuine, this object is reasonably considered as fake. The identification of this "Dual System" is a serious approach should be held in the current academic context. All of the artifacts determined by Dual System as genuine are also authenticated by all of the existing verification methods as genuine and have ruled out any doubts, the current academic and collecting fields failed to provide opposing basis. In this case, the value of the object itself can be determined, by which the room for value growth can also be promised. The ones falsified by the Dual System were because there are suspicious circumstances surrounding the identification of the results obtained, so it is a cautious approach. It does not rule out the feasibility that the objects are actually genuine, but from the view of investment, it may the most effectively avert the risk.

Dual System as the integration of visual verification and the scientific identification is in terms of the method rather than in terms of the experts. It is an integration of various appraising methods, namely the authentication of antique artworks using the existing identification methods, the results of which are cross-checked to exclude the interference of human factors as thoroughly as possible and finally get a proven comprehensive conclusion. Such a result is the guarantee of successful risk averse in the art investment.

The estimation of the art investment to the room of growth of the cultural value of artworks and the expectation to the future markets are achieved by visual identification. Dual System is the double guaranteed identifying method, the visual identification in which includes both the typology and trace studies as well as the predicting of the art market. The experts in the cultural relics and museology fields, the experts of archeology, the experts on antique artwork management, and experienced connoisseurs and collectors all belong to the Dual System; for the art investment to specific cultural works, Dual System will bring together their respective views into a comprehensive reasoning procedure. The result of this reasoning procedure contains a description of the authenticity of the artifacts and the judgments to its market price, value growth and possible risks. The art investment for antique artworks based on this kind of reasoning results is the most rational way of risk aversion under the existing conditions.

现代测试技术在古艺术品鉴定中的应用

郭立鹤

我们向广大藏家介绍使用结构分析测试技术在测定陶瓷釉质老化程度方面取得的进展。

已有研究告诉我们，经高温熔融形成的釉子，是一种玻璃态均质体。在自然环境中，釉子的内部结构是无序的，内应力不均匀，呈亚稳定状态。随着时间的推移，它的内部结构会不断自动地进行调整，由无序的亚稳定状态逐步向有序的稳定状态转变，这就是釉子的老化现象。实际上，釉子的自然老化过程，就是其自发地对局部结构进行调整，内部应力由不平衡逐渐趋于较为平衡的过程。表现形式就是在釉子内部和表面产生微裂纹，其透光性逐渐降低，对光线散射性不断增强。

因此古瓷器的釉面看上去要比新品柔和、温润，时代越久，这种反差就越大。有些品种的古瓷器，因特殊的烧制工艺过程使得釉子的内应力极不均匀，其老化现象还表现为在釉面出现不同形态的微裂纹(俗称"开片")。这种微裂纹有的可以用肉眼直接观察到，有的则要借助现代科学仪器才能发现。

釉子的老化现象，是物质自身内部结构调整的结果，是瓷器自诞生之日起就持续不断发生的一种特有的变化，随着时间的推移，老化程度不断加深，较少受到外界自然环境的影响。使用物理方法或化学方法作旧，主要对釉子表面有一些损伤，对釉子的内部结构影响较少。通过现代物质结构测试技术可以确定釉子结构变化的程度，推测釉子的年代。

对陶瓷釉质老化程度测试的结果表明，目前使用的结构分析技术是成功的，具有快速测量、不损伤艺术品的特点。

物质结构分析是当代发展最快、应用范围最广的一门学科，涉及多种测试技术，可以提供多方面的信息。结构老化分析只是众多结构分析的内容之一，结构老化现象不仅发生在瓷釉上，丝、绸、布、帛、纸张、料器等等都有老化的问题，我们计划在今后逐步开展有关研究工作。

希望古老的艺术品研究鉴定界能够吸收更多的现代分析测试技术。

·作者为中国地质科学院矿产资源研究所研究员。

The Application of Modern Testing Techniques on the Identification of Ancient Artworks

Guo Lihe

Here, we introduce the developments of the structural analysis technique on the testing of the aging degree of the ceramic glazes to the collectors.

The past researches told us that the glaze formed by high temperature is a kind of vitreous isotropic body. In natural environments, the internal structure of the glaze is disordered, its internal stress is uneven and in a metastable state. As time goes by, its internal structure is automatically rearranging, adjusting and changing from the disordered metastable state to ordered stable state, which is called the aging of the glaze. In fact, the natural aging process of the glaze is that for the glaze to regulate its own internal structure, and for its internal stress to get evener and evener. The demonstration of this process is that tiny cracks are emerging from the inside and surface of the glaze, causing the reducing of the transparency and the increasing of the light scattering ability.

Therefore, the glaze of the ancient ceramics are looking much more gentle and slender than that of the new products, and the longer the time gap is, the larger the contrast will be. Some kinds of ancient ceramics, because of the special burning technique and procedure, the internal stress of their glaze was very uneven, which made their aging as crackles in varying shapes, which are called Kaipian. Some of the crackles can be observed directly with naked eyes and some of them are only seen through the assistance of modern scientific instruments.

The aging of the glaze is the result of the internal adjusting of the structure of the materials and a constant changing process peculiar to the ceramics when it was born. Along with the time elapses, the aging degree is also deepening, and it is seldom influenced by external environments. The artificial aging techniques with physical or chemical methods can only damage the surface of the glaze but can hardly reach the internal structure. The modern structural analysis technique can identify the grades of the changes of the internal structure of the glaze and estimate its date.

The results of the tests to the aging degree of the ceramic glazes show that the structural analysis technique used at present is successful. It works quickly and does not damage the artworks.

Material structure analysis is a rapidly developing and widely applied technique in modern times. It integrates many testing techniques and can provide information of many aspects. Aging degree analysis is only one of the many contents of the structure analysis. The aging process happens not only on ceramic glaze but also on silks and other textiles, paper and glasses, and we are planning to expand our work on them in the future.

We hope that the artwork identification field with long history can absorb more modern techniques.

Guo Lihe, who graduated in Geochemistry Specialty, Department of Geology and Geography, Peking University in 1964, was a research fellow of Institute of Mineral Resources, Chinese Academy of Geological Sciences before retirement, where his research interests were the spectroscopy of mineral materials and inorganic materials and their applications. At present, he is working on the researches and developments of spectroscopic testing techniques of gemstones and ceramic glazes.

清代中晚期官窑瓷器拍卖行情观察

阮富春

图1 清嘉庆黄地粉彩福寿万年云口瓶

图2 清道光青花粉彩十八罗汉图扁方瓶

随着中国经济的持续飞速发展，艺术品市场的交易越来越活跃，收藏者、投资者群体急速扩大，尤其是中国内地，艺术品市场的发展速度居全球之首。以拍卖高端中国文物艺术精品的香港市场为例，到2010年春拍时，参与香港苏富比、佳士得两大拍卖公司的内地买家已经达到了两公司全部买家的50%。中国内地收藏者、投资者的收藏品位，已经开始左右着全球范围内中国艺术品交易的行情风向。

从全球艺术品市场来看，中国艺术品具有国际性身份的首列瓷器，这与历代瓷器外销海外所产生的持久影响力关系密切。欧美市场、中国市场的收藏者在瓷器的年代取向上有一定区别：欧美藏家较青睐唐、宋、元时代的高古陶器、瓷器，而中国区域内则推崇明清官窑瓷器。20世纪早期到80年代末期，中国老一辈瓷器收藏家注重宋元名瓷及明代官窑精品的收藏，而随着高古名瓷数量大幅减少，香港、台湾地区新一代进入收藏市场的收藏者、投资人士将视角投向了华美、漂亮的清代瓷器，特别是清三代官窑瓷成了他们极力搜求的对象。时至今日，清三代官窑精品已经成为中国天价瓷器的代名词，乾隆宫廷御制的瓷器精品目前单件的最高交易价格已达5.5亿元——2010年11月11日，伦敦郊区米尔德塞克斯小镇班布里奇（Bainbridge）拍卖行上拍出一件清乾隆时期的粉彩镂空瓷瓶，传说被中国内地买家以5160万英镑拍得。即便是在中国市场，去年香港苏富比秋拍中，一件清乾隆浅黄地洋彩锦上添花万寿连延图长颈葫芦瓶的交易价也达到了2.5266亿港币。目前清三代官窑精品的成交价动辄超过千万元，中等品的成交价也在数百万元。

历代瓷器精品在全球范围内行情的走高，对推动艺术品市场整体的行情发展功不可没，但同时也加大了瓷器收藏者的投入成本，动辄千万元甚至亿元的价格，提高了入场的门槛，也限制了很大一部分收藏者。在这样的市场背景下，瓷器收藏者有必要对瓷器板块进行"深耕细作"，深入发掘未来的潜力品种。因此，清代中晚期瓷器自然成了关注的焦点。毕竟，清代自顺治始至宣统朝268年间，清三代134年仅占了一半，除去顺治18年，嘉庆至宣统占到了116年，就瓷器的研究、收藏而言，这116年是不可轻易忽视的，尤其是嘉庆、道光、同治、光绪四朝的瓷器。

事实证明，市场上早就出现了先知先觉者，香港、台湾、内地早已出现了一大批涉足清代中晚期官窑瓷器精品的收藏者，他们在其他藏家尚沉浸于追捧清三代的热潮时，已经在悄然收藏清代中晚期瓷器，就笔者所知，一些收藏者的藏品已经相当成规模。笔者近年来持续观察清代中晚期瓷器的拍卖行情，嘉庆、道光、同治、光绪四朝的官窑精品价格飙升迹象明显。

首先是嘉庆、道光官窑瓷器精品行情走高。早在2007年8月中贸圣佳推出"嘉庆宫廷艺术品专场"时，曾经英国苏格兰阿伯丁郡英韦卡特城堡（Invercauld Castle，Aberdeenshire）、弗格阿瑞森（Captain Farguharson's）收藏过的清嘉庆粉彩进宝图螭耳瓶就拍出了1019.2万元。2010年嘉庆瓷器再创新高，2件成交价超千万元：19世纪英国富豪阿尔弗雷特·莫里森（Alfred Morrison）家族放山居（Fonthill House）收藏的清嘉庆黄地粉彩福寿万年云口瓶（图1），在香港佳士得拍到了9026万港币；日本藏家收藏、2008年香港苏富比春拍释出的清嘉庆青花海水九龙葫芦瓶，在北京保利秋拍中也拍到了1344万元。也有行家认为，这类工艺精细的嘉庆瓷即有可能是乾隆退位后做太上皇时期的制品。但无论如何，嘉庆瓷器行情的上涨无疑推动了清代中晚期瓷器的价格上升。

其实早在20世纪90年代中期，一些有远见的收藏家便已经在关注道光官窑瓷器，并且开始了专题性质的收藏，当下北京、山西、浙江等地不乏收藏大家。北京诚轩拍卖公司瓷杂部经理戴岱曾指出，"道光瓷的专题藏家远多于嘉庆瓷专家，原因是嘉庆瓷器风格上还是属于乾隆时期的延续，而道光瓷器另具特点，生产的品种和数量也远比嘉庆瓷多。有一定的数量，才能吸引藏家。"2005年以来，拍场上由于明清盛世官窑瓷器越来越难寻，道光瓷器开始走俏，价格大幅上涨。2006年北京翰海秋拍319万元成

图3 清道光粉彩仙人祝寿方瓶

图4 清道光粉彩三羊开泰图双象耳瓶

图5 清道光黄地粉彩花卉五福宫碗（一对）

图6 清咸丰粉彩八仙人物图双蝠耳瓶

图7 清同治青花缠枝花卉赏瓶

图8 清光绪绿釉开光雕鱼龙变化纹双耳瓶（一对）

交的"慎德堂制"款青花粉彩十八罗汉图扁方瓶（图2），1997年出现于该公司春季大拍时，成交价仅33万元，9年时间，价格上涨接近十倍。2007年北京翰海春拍302.4万元成交的粉彩仙人祝寿方瓶（图3），曾是1995年中国嘉德春拍瓷杂专场的封面拍品，底书"慎德堂制"二行四字楷书红款，为道光朝的御瓷精品，当时估价15万至25万元，以20.9万元成交，12年时间，增值近15倍。同年中贸圣佳夏拍，高67.5厘米、署"慎德堂制"楷书红款的清道光粉彩三羊开泰图双象耳瓶也拍出了336万元（图4）。

2010年香港苏富比、佳士得秋拍的两场私人收藏专拍中，分别有2件道光瓷器成交价创道光瓷价格之最：戴润斋旧藏的1对清道光粉彩仿剔红雕漆锦地万福图盖罐以782万港币拍出；放山居收藏的1对清道光黄地粉彩花卉五福宫碗以662万港币易主（图5），可见道光瓷器精品的价格已经不低。1840年鸦片战争的爆发，将中国历史拉入了近代，生产力下降，虽然道光一朝瓷器远不如前，但还是有不少工艺水平较高的瓷器。中国市场上道光瓷器2001年价格才过百万元，十年来，价超百万元的不足60件。

长期以来，不少研究者、收藏人士认为同治、光绪时期景德镇制瓷数量巨大，工艺粗劣，因此这两朝瓷器长期不受重视，以致专门研究成果缺乏，也不受市场关注。事实上，这是非常没有远见的。同治朝历13年，而光绪一朝历时长达34年，仅次于康熙、乾隆两朝，瓷器生产的数量、品种不容小视。就市场来看，当前咸丰、同治、光绪和宣统四朝官窑瓷器的拍卖价格仍然在低谷徘徊。但若从历年这四朝瓷器的行情走势看，2006年以来的涨幅却也相当惊人，特别是一些在市场上流传有绪的精品，每次出现价格必定翻番，甚至上涨数倍。咸丰瓷器流通量少而价格较高，官窑精品近年来的最高成交价也超过了百万元。2007年中国嘉德春拍，清咸丰粉彩八仙人物图双蝠耳瓶曾拍出80.64万元（图6）。2009年北京匡时与日本亲和在香港秋拍时，清咸丰粉彩喜字双联瓶拍出了207万港币。同治瓷器的流通量远大于咸丰瓷，成交价格低于咸丰瓷。同治、光绪瓷器的交易行情前些年长期波澜不惊，但是近两年突然变化明显，以2010年最具代表性。2010年北京翰海秋拍，同治时期的一件青花缠枝花卉赏瓶估18万至28

万元（图7），结果拍到了78.4万元，是中国市场目前最贵的一件同治瓷器。目前同治瓷器精品的稳定价格大约在50万元左右，一般品价格只是一二十万元。

光绪瓷器历年上拍的数量最大，品种非常丰富，精品的成交价已超过200万元，是晚清几朝瓷器中的主流拍品。相对清三代瓷器而言，道光、同治、光绪三朝瓷器的价格较低，因此瓷器收藏者近年来纷纷将视角转移到了这一板块上。有业内人士指出，与清三代瓷器的市场不同，晚清三代瓷器因当前市场价位普遍不高，香港市场上拍的数量较少，中心市场主要在中国内地，对于内地藏家而言可供选择的余地较大。同时，在拍卖公司的推介和知名藏家的引导下，未来晚清官窑瓷器的价格将会出现一轮新的利好行情。

图9 清光绪"储秀宫制"款黄釉地粉彩"万寿无疆"纹大盘

光绪官窑瓷器的烧制达到了晚清最高水平，拍场上的成交价及涨幅也最高。1996年北京翰海春拍时，一对"大清光绪年制"款绿釉开光雕鱼龙变化纹双耳瓶拍出了77万元（图8），2006年该公司秋拍时成交价涨至209万元。2002年光绪官窑瓷器的成交价突破百万元大关——上海敬华春拍，直径71.2厘米的光绪时期"储秀宫制"款黄釉地粉彩"万寿无疆"纹大盘创出了110万元（图9）。大盘拍前估50万至60万元，出自上海文物商店旧藏，1994年曾被收入《清代瓷器赏鉴》一书。储秀宫是当时慈禧太后的寝宫，从瓷盘所用的大量黄色及"万寿无疆"饰纹来看，应是慈禧所用瓷器。

图10 清光绪"大雅斋"款黄地粉彩喜鹊登梅图大碗

光绪瓷器的价格缘何居晚清瓷器之首？这与当时景德镇瓷器烧制的复兴有重要的因果关系。同治十年（1871年）出生的光绪皇帝，其母是慈禧之妹，1875年光绪即位，慈禧仍然主导着朝政。1875年至1908年，光绪帝在位34年，在清朝十帝中仅次于在位61年的康熙帝和60年的乾隆帝，历史学者将光绪朝称为封建王朝的回光反照。因太平军和捻军起义被平息，光绪时期社会秩序相对进入到了一个所谓"同光中兴"的平稳期。瓷器生产方面，在光绪大婚、慈禧六十大寿、七十大寿等重要喜事的推动下，上行下效，烧制数量之多，品种之全，达到了乾隆以后的盛期。如光绪二十年，为慈禧"万寿节"烧制瓷器花费白银就达129963.435两。

图11 清光绪青花"天下第一泉"字坛

从档案记载及传世器物来看，光绪瓷器基本上囊括了大部分的传统器型，既有仿古也有创新。清宫档案记载，自光绪元年至光绪三十四年，景德镇始终没有停止过大规模的瓷器烧制。瓷器研究专家认为，此时期烧制的慈禧御用"大雅斋"款官窑瓷器，是本朝比较少见的精品。常见器型有大缸、花盆、碗、盘、盒等等，"多是在蓝色、浅青色、藕荷色、浅紫色的地子上淡墨彩绘，画风细柔，图案精巧"。器物上有"大雅斋"三字款，以及"天地一家春"、"永庆升平"、"永庆长春"等闲章。装饰纹饰题材多样，以藤萝花鸟、鹭鸶莲花、葡萄花鸟等最为常见。2002年北京翰海秋拍时，清光绪"大雅斋"款的黄地粉彩喜鹊登梅图大碗就拍出了15.4万元（图10）。

图12 清宣统粉彩麻姑献寿瓶

光绪时期景德镇仿古瓷器的生产也达到了乾隆以后的最高峰，仿康熙、乾隆两朝瓷器最多，以仿康熙青花瓷成就最高。有学者认为，仿古瓷的大量烧造，与上层社会对清三代瓷器的好古风尚相关。虽然是仿古，但是制瓷的手工绘制水平也达到了一定的高度，形成了本朝独特的艺术风格，纹饰丰富多彩，装饰华丽生动。《饮流斋说瓷》中有"而光绪近年仿康、乾诸制往往逼真，鱼目混珠，识者憎之，然不能不谓其美术之精进也"的记载。有研究者指出，光绪朝仿乾隆粉彩瓷的器物胎釉细致缜密，工艺精湛，最具代表性的是粉彩九桃大瓶、百鹿尊等琢器。此时期新创烧的器型也不少，比如秋操纪念杯、云蝠赏瓶等。釉彩方面仍以粉彩、青花及单色釉为主流，也出现不少新釉彩品种，如浅绛彩。光绪朝瓷器的款识种类也居晚清几朝之首，除常见的干支年款外，堂名款也较多，其中以"长春宫制"、"一善堂"、"慎德堂制"、"退思斋"、"春怡堂制"、"甘泽堂制"等款识的瓷器制作较精。

图13 清宣统粉彩花卉玉壶春瓶

粉彩、单色釉瓷之外，历年成交价最高的光绪青花瓷器也超过了百万元。2005年香港佳士得春拍时，高40.7厘米的青花"天下第一泉"字坛以96万港币成交（图11）。这种盖罐早在1995年中国嘉德春拍时，曾创下55万元的成交价。盖罐盘口、短颈、溜肩、圆腹、圈足，足内青花书"大清光绪年制"楷款。有意思的是，盖罐的肩部以篆书题写"天下第一泉"四个大字，罐腹以青花书馆阁体乾隆御制诗《御制试中冷泉作》全文。有藏家认为，当时这种罐是为慈禧饮水而烧制的，所盛的泉水是每日从北京西郊玉泉山运来的。当然，这仅是现代人根据记载的一种推测，但却给这种瓷器平添了些许传奇。

光绪瓷器存世量大，近年来上拍的数量也日渐增多，据笔者大略统计，中国市场历年成交价超过百万元以上有十余件，大部分都在近两年创出。有藏家认为，嘉道以后，光绪瓷器因为量大，收藏起来比较容易成专题，将是未来晚清官窑瓷器收藏中的一个潜在热点。2010年北京地区拍出了3件超百万元器，器型都较大。北京保利秋拍1对清光绪御制黄地粉彩百鸟朝凤大瓶以246.4万元居历年之首，对瓶高140厘米，原是民国时期上海巨贾叶澄衷之子叶贻铨旧藏品，后归上海友谊商店。该公司春拍还以109.76万元拍出一组美国藏家旧藏的六扇屏清光绪仿珐琅彩二十四孝瓷板。北京翰海秋拍，底书"储秀宫制"篆书款的清光绪黄地彩云龙大盘以112万元拍出。近年来，较好的光绪瓷器价格大多在六七十万元。

宣统帝溥仪在位仅三年清朝的封建历史就落下了帷幕，以前有人认为这三年烧造的瓷器数量少，质量也差。但是据陶瓷专家研究，事实并非如此。从档案记载来看，宣统元年、宣统二年都曾烧制了大量的瓷器——"宣统元年烧造上色圆琢器8594件，次色圆琢器18002件，破损圆琢器5745件，实际报销银两19803.945两；宣统二年烧造上色圆琢器2066件，次色圆琢器5150件，破损圆琢器1740件，实际报销银两10990.086两。"因缺少宣统三年的生产档案，无法统计清朝最后一年的瓷器生产情况。但从宣统前两年的数据看，御窑厂烧制的成品数量远在4万件以上。

目前拍卖市场上宣统瓷器的价格虽然仍处在低谷，但2010年的表现却令人瞩目，一年里中国市场成交价超过30万元的多达十余件，数量和价格均创历年之最。香港佳士得春拍时，先后由养志堂、景艺堂收藏过的清宣统粉彩麻姑献寿瓶拍出了122万港币（图12），是目前拍场上最贵的一件宣统瓷器。秋拍时，该公司上拍的清宣统青花胭脂红八仙过海纹碗也拍出了92万港币。拍场上常见书"大清宣统年制"六字款的碗、

图14　清宣统青花竹石芭蕉玉壶春瓶

赏瓶、玉壶春瓶，以粉彩、五彩、青花器为主。早在2000年北京翰海春拍时，粉彩花卉的玉壶春瓶成交价已达22.55万元（图13）。2005年该公司秋拍时，一件宣统的青花竹石芭蕉玉壶春瓶的成交价达41.8万元（图14）。

综合清瓷板块的行情可以看出，雍正、乾隆瓷器的价格已经到了相当的高度了，非寻常收藏者所能承受，接随着嘉庆瓷器价格的飙升，清中期、清晚期瓷器的行情将全线飘红，未来这一板块将会引人瞩目。

· 本文作于2011年年初，统计数据不包含2011年春拍。作者阮富春，为《文物天地》杂志编辑。

The Observation to the Auction Market of theMid and Late Qing Official Kiln Porcelains

Ruan Fuchun

With the sustained and rapid development of China's economy, the art market is getting more and more dynamic, the populations of collectors and investors of which are also rapidly expanding, especially in mainland China, the art market's growth rate of which ranks first in the world. In the Hong Kong art market, where is the trading center of high-end Chinese cultural relics and artworks, the mainland buyers attending the 2010 Spring Auction run by Sotheby's and Christie's have reached 50% of all buyers. The collecting interests and tastes of the mainland collectors and investors have begun to dominate the global trade market of Chinese artworks.

Seen from the global art market, the top-ranked Chinese artworks having international identity could be the porcelains, which is tightly related to their long-lasting influence caused by the exporting in the past centuries. In the international and domestic art markets, Chinese porcelain collection orientations have certain time difference: the porcelains and potteries made in the Tang, Song and Yuan Dynasties, which are called High-antique Ceramics, are more popular in the European and American collectors. The Chinese collectors, on the other hand, are more interested in the porcelains made in the Ming and Qing Dynasties. Since the early 20th century to the late 1980s, the older generation of Chinese porcelain collectors focused more on the Song and Yuan porcelains and the fine products of the official kilns of the Ming Dynasty. Along with the substantially decreasing of the fine samples of high-antique ceramics, in Hong Kong and Taiwan, the new generation of collectors in the art market turned their attention to the gorgeous and exquisite Qing porcelains, especially those of the official kilns of the Three-era Period (Kangxi, Yongzheng and Qianlong Eras, 1662-1795) of the Qing Dynasty have become the objects of their eager art searching. Today, the fine products of the official kilns of the Three-era Period of the Qing Dynasty has almost become

Figure 1, Jiaqing, Qing, the Yellow-ground Famille-rose Vase with Cloud-shaped Rim and the "Endless Happiness and Longevity" (Intertwined Lotus Branches and Flowers, Bats and Ribbons) Motif.

Figure 2, Daoguang, Qing, the Blue-and-white Rectangular Vase with the Famille-rose Figures of the Eighteen Arhats.

the synonym of the Chinese porcelains with sky-high prices: the highest hammer price of a single masterpiece of the Qianlong official kiln product has reached 550 million CNY - on November 11, 2010, a Qianlong famille-rose porcelain vase with openwork decoration was purchased by a Chinese mainland buyer with "a record breaking bid" of £51.6 million at Bainbridge Auction in Middlesex, a small town in London suburb. Even in the Chinese market, in the Autumn Auction of Hong Kong Sotheby's last year, a Qianlong long-necked gourd-shaped vase with foreign enamel light-yellow-ground, brocade ground design and "Blessing Longevity" motif was also sold at a price as high as 252.66 million HKD. At present, the close prices of fine products of the official kilns of the Three-era Period of the Qing Dynasty were very easily reaching prices of dozens of millions of CNY, even those pieces of medium and mean qualities could also be sold at millions of CNY.

That the fine porcelain products are getting higher and higher prices on the art market worldwide contributed greatly to promoting the overall art market development, but also increased the input costs of those porcelain collectors. The scaring prices as high as tens even hundreds of millions of CNY heightened the admission threshold of porcelain collecting, and limited a large part of collectors. In this market context, it is necessary for the porcelain collectors to "closely cultivate and finely sow" the "porcelain block" to further explore the potential varieties in the future. Therefore, the porcelains made in the late Qing Dynasty naturally became the focus of attention. After all, the Qing Dynasty lasted 268 years from the Shunzhi to Xuantong Eras, in which the "Three-era Period" lasting for 134 years took only a half, if we exclude the 18 years of Shunzhi Era, the time block of the Qing Dynasty from Jiaqing to Xuantong Eras accounted for 116 years, which should not be overlooked for the researches and collecting of porcelains, especially the Jiaqing, Daoguang, Tongzhi

Figure 3, Daoguang, Qing, the Famille-rose Rectangular Vase with "Immortals Congratulating Birthday" Motif.

and Guangxu Eras.

Facts have proved that prophets have long emerged in the art market. A large group of collectors in Hong Kong, Taiwan and the mainland have long been involved in the collecting of the fine porcelains of the late Qing Dynasty. When the other collectors were still absorbed in the pursuit of the "Three-era" porcelains, they had quietly turned to the seeking of the late Qing porcelains. As my knowledge, some of the collectors have built their collections into a quite large scale. In recent years, I have continued to observe the auction market of the late Qing porcelains, and noticed that the prices of the fine official kiln products of the Jiaqing, Daoguang, Tongzhi and Guangxu Eras have been clearly boomed.

First, the prices of the fine products of the official kilns of the Jiaqing and Daoguang Eras created one new height after another. Back in mid-August 2007, when the Sungari International Auction Company launched the "Court Art of Jiaqing Special Auction", a famille-rose vase with hornless dragon-shaped handles and "Presenting Treasures" motif, which had been collected by the Invercauld Castle, Aberdeen Shire and Captain Farquharson was sold at the price as high as 10.192 million CNY. In 2010, Jiaqing porcelains created a new height: two of them were sold at over ten million CNY: a yellow-ground famille-rose vase with cloud-shaped rim and the "Endless Happiness and Longevity" (intertwined lotus branches and flowers, bats and ribbons) motif (Figure 1), which had been collected by Alfred Morrison, a British rich of the 19th century in his family's Fonthill House, was sold in Hong Kong Christie's at the high price of 90.26 million HKD. A blue-and-white double-gourd-shaped vase with sea wave pattern and nine dragon motifs, which had been collected by a Japanese connoisseur and released on the 2008 Spring Auction of Hong Kong Sotheby's was sold at a price of 13.44 million CNY on the Beijing Poly

Figure 4, Daoguang, Qing, the Famille-rose Vase with Double Elephant-shaped Handles and "Three-ram" (the Beginning of Good Fortune) Motif.

Figure 5, Daoguang, Qing, the Yellow-ground Famille-rose "Palace Bowls" with Floral Patterns on the Outer Wall and "Five Good Fortunes (Bats)" Motif on the Inner Bottom (a Pair).

Autumn Auction. There are experts believing that the Jiaqing porcelains showing such sophisticated technology might have been made for Emperor Qianlong after he abdicated the throne to Emperor Jiaqing. Nevertheless, the rise in prices of Jiaqing porcelain is undoubtedly promoted that of the late Qing porcelains.

In fact, as early as in the mid-1990s, some far-sighted collectors have been already concerned about the Daoguang official kiln porcelains, and begun the collection with them as the subject. At present, famous collectors of Daoguang official kiln porcelains can be seen in Beijing, Shanxi, Zhejiang and other places. Mr. Dai Dai, who is the manager of the department of ceramics and miscellany of Beijing Chengxuan Auction Company, has pointed out, "the subject collectors on Daoguang porcelains are far more than that on Jiaqing porcelains, because Jiaqing porcelains were still succeeding the styles of Qianlong porcelains but the Daoguang porcelains had their own characteristics, and their quantities and types are also far more than that of Jiaqing porcelains. To attract collectors, a good quantity is necessary." Since 2005, because the porcelains of the Golden Ages of the Ming and Qing Dynasties were more and more difficult to find in the art markets, the Daoguang porcelains began to win better and better market and get higher and higher prices. On the 2006 Autumn Auction of Beijing Hanhai Auction Company, a blue-and-white rectangular vase with the famille-rose figures of the Eighteen Arhats and "Shende Tang" (Shende Studio, see Figure 2) seal mark was sold at the hammer price as high as 3.19 million CNY. However, when it appeared on the 1997 Spring Auction of the same company, it had been sold at a hammer price of only 330 thousand CNY. During the nine years, its price rose for almost ten times. On the 2007 Spring Auction of Beijing Hanhai Auction Company, a famille-rose rectangular vase with "Immortals Congratulating Birthday" motif (Figure 3)

Figure 6, Xianfeng, Qing, the Famille-rose Vase with Figures of the Eight Immortals and Double Bat-shaped Handles.

was sold at the hammer price of 3.024 million CNY. It had been the front cover lot of the 1995 Spring Special Event of Ceramics and Miscellany of Guardian Auction House because it was a masterpiece of Daoguang official kiln bearing the "Shende Tang Made" seal mark in red color and in regular script on the bottom. However, at that time, its price was estimated as between 150 to 250 thousand CNY and finally sold at the hammer price of 209 thousand CNY. In the 12 years, its price increased almost 15 times. On the Summer Auction of Sungari International Auction Company of the same year, a 67.5 cm high "Shende Tang Made" famille-rose vase with double elephant-shaped handles and "Three-ram (the beginning of good fortune)" motif was also sold at a hammer price of 3.36 million CNY (Figure 4).

In 2010, on the two special events for private collection auction held by Hong Kong Sotheby's and Christie's in their Autumn Auctions, two pairs of Daoguang porcelains created new bid price heights: a pair of famille-rose lidded jars with imitation carved lacquer brocade pattern and "Ten Thousand Good Fortunes" (flying bats) motif, which had ever been collected by J. T. Tai were sold at the hammer price of 7.82 million HKD, a pair of yellow-ground famille-rose "Palace Bowls" with floral patterns on the outer wall and "Five Good Fortunes (bats)" motif on the inner bottom, which had ever been collected by Alfred Morrison in his family's Fonthill House (Figure 5) were sold at the hammer price of 6.62 million HKD. These two events reflected that the prices of the fine Daoguang porcelains on art market have reached a rather high level. The outbreak of the Opium War in 1840 pulled China into the modern time and the productivity decreased; although the Daoguang porcelains are far less in quantity and quality than that of the past, there still were many porcelain products showing sophisticated craftsmanship. In 2001, the highest price of Daoguang porcelain on the art market began to surpass one million CNY. In

Figure 7. Tongzhi, Qing, the Blue-and-white Awarding Vase with Intertwined Floral Designs.

Figure 8. Guangxu, Qing, the Green-glazed Vases with Medallion Engraved Fish-dragon Transformation Motif and Double Handles (a Pair).

Figure 9, Guangxu, Qing, the Yellow-ground Famille-rose Plate with "Wan Shou Wu Jiang (Eternal Longevity)" Characters Motif and "Made for Chuxiu Hall" Seal Mark.

the 10 years since, no more than 60 pieces of Daoguang porcelains with estimated prices more than one million have appeared.

Over the years, many researchers and collectors believed that in the Tongzhi and Guangxu Eras, the porcelains made in Jingdezhen were in huge amount and poor techniques, so the porcelains ot these two eras have been neglected or looked down upon for rather long time, resulting in a lack of dedicated researches and concerned markets. In fact, this is very shortsighted. Tongzhi Era lasted for 13 years and Guangxu lasted 34 years, second only to Kangxi and Qianlong Eras, and the quantities and varieties of the porcelains produced in these two eras cannot be overlooked. Seen from the present art market, the bid prices of the official kiln porcelains of Xianfeng, Tongzhi, Guangxu and Xuantong Eras are still hovering at the bottom. However, from the market trends of the porcelains of these four eras, the increase since 2006 is also quite amazing, especially the fine ones with clear provenances, every time when they appear on the market, their prices will double, or even several times higher. The porcelains made in Xianfeng Era are usually in higher prices because of their small quantity in art markets. The official kiln products with high quality of which also surpassed one million CNY in recent years. On the 2007 Spring Auction of Beijing Guardian Auction House, a famille-rose vase with figures of the Eight Immortals and double bat-shaped handles was sold at the hammer price of 806.4 thousand CNY (Figure 6). On the Autumn Auction held by Beijing Council International Auction Company and Japan Shinwa Art Auction in Hong Kong, a famille-rose joint vase with Double-Xi (Happiness) character motif was sold at the hammer price of 2.07 million HKD. The porcelains made in Tongzhi Era are larger in quantity on the art markets, and their closing prices are usually lower than Xianfeng porcelains. The markets of Tongzhi and Guangxu porcelains have been rather stable in several years ago. However, the situation suddenly and apparently changed in the past two years, and the markets in 2010 was the most representative. In the 2010 Autumn Auction of Beijing Hanhai Auction Company, a blue-and-white awarding vase with intertwined floral designs had been estimated to 180 to 280 thousand CNY (Figure 7), but the last hammer price reached 784 thousand CNY, which is the most expensive Tongzhi porcelain in the mainland art market. The stable prices of fine Tongzhi porcelains are around 0.5 million CNY each piece, and that of the common quality are only 0.1 to 0.2 million.

The porcelains made in the Guangxu Era appear in large quantities and abundant varieties in art auctions of the recent years, and the closing prices of the fine ones of them have surpassed two million CNY each piece. Guangxu porcelains is the mainstream of the late Qing porcelains in auction market. Compared to the so-called "Three-era" porcelains, the porcelains made in Daoguang, Tongzhi and Guangxu Eras are relatively cheap, so the porcelain collectors in recent years have shifted their view to this plate. Insiders have pointed out that different from the "Three-era" porcelains, the main market of the porcelains of the three eras of the late Qing Dynasty is in mainland: because their prices are generally low, these porcelains seldom appear in the auction markets of Hong Kong, and therefore the mainland collectors have larger choice room. Meanwhile, with the promotion of the auction companies and the guidance of well-known collectors, the official kiln products of the late Qing Dynasty will earn a new good market.

Figure 10, Guangxu, Qing, the Yellow-ground Famille-rose "Da Ya Zhai" Bowl with "Magpies Perching on Plum Branch" Motif.

The official kiln porcelain of Guangxu Era reached the climax of the craftsmanship in the late Qing Dynasty, and their prices and rate of rise are also the highest in auction markets. In the 1996 Spring Auction of Beijing Hanhai Auction Company, a pair of green-glazed vases with medallion engraved fish-dragon transformation motif and double handles and "Made in Guangxu Era" seal mark (Figure 8) were sold at the hammer price of 770 thousand CNY. When they appeared again in the 2006 Autumn Auction of the same company, the hammer price increased to 2.09 million. In 2002, the closing prices of Guangxu official kiln products began to exceed one million CNY: in the 2002 Spring Auction of Shanghai Jinghua Art Auction Company, a yellow-ground famille-rose plate 71.2 cm in diameter with "Wan Shou Wu Jiang" (Eternal Longevity) characters as motif and "Made for Chuxiu Hall" seal mark (Figure 9) was sold at the hammer price of 1.1 million CNY, while its estimated price before the auction was only 500 to 600 thousand. It had been stored in Shanghai Antique Shop and cataloged into the Qingdai Ciqi Shangjian (the Connoisseurship of the Porcelains of the Qing Dynasty) in 1994. Chuxiu Hall was the Empress Dowager Cixi's sleeping quarters, the yellow color and the "Wan Shou Wu Jiang" motif of this plate implied that it would have been used by Cixi.

Figure 11. Guangxu, Qing, the Blue-and-white Jar with "Tianxia Diyi Quan" Poem Inscription.

Why do the prices of Guangxu porcelains top that of the late Qing Dynasty? It is tightly related to the revival of the Jingdezhen porcelain industry. The mother of Emperor Guangxu (born in the tenth year of Tongzhi Era, 1871) was the sister of Empress Dowager Cixi, when Emperor Guangxu ascended the throne in 1875, Empress Dowager Cixi was continuing to dominate the affairs of the state. Guangxu Era lasted for 34 years from 1875 to 1908, only second to the reigns of Emperors Kangxi (61 years) and Qianlong (60 years), and historians called it as the "last glow of the setting sun" of the Qing Empire. Because the Taiping and Nian uprisings were over, the social order during the Guangxu Era entered into a stable period called "Tongzhi-Guangxu Restoration". Because of the imperial bridal and the Empress Dowager Cixi's sixtieth and seventieth birthdays and other important events and ceremonies, the porcelain production was driven onto a new peak: the quantities, qualities and varieties of the porcelains of this period were all the highest since the Qianlong Era. In the 20th year of Guangxu Era, up to 129,963.435 teals of silver had been spent on the porcelain producing for the "Longevity Festival" (the sixtieth birthday) of Empress Dowager Cixi.

Seen from the historic archives and the handed down artifacts, Guangxu porcelains generally covered most of the traditional types, both antique imitative and innovative. As the records of the Qing court archives, during the entire Guangxu Era, in the thirty-four years, Jingdezhen has never stopped large-scale porcelain producing. Porcelain expert believes that the "Da Ya Zhai" (Great Elegance Studio) official kiln porcelains made for Empress Dowager Cixi were rare masterpieces of this period. The popular types are big jars, flower pots, bowls, plates, cases, etc. "The motifs are mostly painted with light ink on blue, light blue, lavender or light purple grounds, the painting styles are gentle and the designs are delicate." The porcelains are usually bearing the three-character "Da Ya Zhai" seal mark, which was the studio name of the producer, and sometimes the leisure stamps such as "Tian Di Yijia Chun" (a hall name in the Old Summer Palace), "Yong Qing Shengping" (Enjoying the Peace and Prosperity forever), "Yong Qing Chang Chun" (Enjoying the Evergreen - Longevity forever), etc. The decoration themes are diverse, the main ones of which are Chinese wisteria and birds, egrets and lotus, grapes and birds, etc. In the 2002 Autumn Auction of Beijing Hanhai Auction Company, a yellow-ground famille-rose "Da Ya Zhai" bowl with "Magpies Perching on Plum Branch" (Figure 10) motif was sold at the hammer price of 154 thousand CNY.

In Guangxu Era, the imitation antique porcelain production in Jingdezhen also reached the peak after Qianlong Era, most of them were the imitations of the

Figure 12. Xuantong, Qing, the Famille-rose Vase with "Magu Presenting Longevity" Motif.

Figure 13. Xuantong, Qing, the Famille-rose Yuhuchun Vase with Floral Designs.

products of Kangxi and Qianlong Eras, the best ones of which are the imitations of Kangxi blue-and-white porcelains. Some scholars believe that the production of large amount of imitation antique porcelains was related to the favorite of the elite societies to the porcelains of the "Three-era Period". Although they are imitation antiques, the painting skill of these porcelains also showed a rather high artistic level, forming a unique style of the Guangxu Era. The patterns are colorful and diversified and the decorations are ornate and vivid. It is said in Yinliu Zhai Shuo Ci (Essays on Porcelains Written in "Drinking-stream Studio") that "in recent years of Guangxu Era, the porcelains imitating that of Kangxi and Qianlong Eras are made true to life and cannot be identified from the genuine ones, which is loathed by the fans of genuine wares; however, we have to recognize their sophisticated art." Some researchers have pointed out that Guangxu's imitation of the famille-rose porcelains of Qianlong Era showed fine textures of bodies and glazes and meticulous workmanship, the most representative ones of which are the large famille-rose "Nine-peach" vases and the "One Hundred-deer" zun-jars and other alike exquisite wares. The newly created types of this period are also many, such as the "Autumn Maneuver Souvenir" cups, awarding vases with cloud-and-dragon and bat designs, etc. The glazes were still famille-rose, blue-and-white and monochrome as the mainstream, but some new glaze varieties also emerged, such as light-crimson, etc. The inscription types of Guangxu porcelains also topped in the late Qing, in addition to the common date (represented by the way of stems-and-branches) marks, the names of studios were also more than that of other eras, of which the ones bearing "Changchun Gong", "Yi Shan Tang", "Shende Studio", "Tui Si Zhai", "Chun Yi Tang", "Ganze Tang" are more delicate than the other porcelains.

In addition to the famille-rose and monochrome glazed porcelains, the highest closing price of Guangxu blue-and-white porcelain also has exceeded one million CNY. In the 2005 Spring Auction of Hong Kong Christie's, a 40.7 cm high blue-and-white porcelain jar with "Tianxia Diyi Quan" poem inscription (Figure 11) was sold at the hammer price of 0.96 million HKD. In the 1995 Spring Auction of Guardian Auction House, its closing price was 550 thousand CNY. This jar has a dish-shaped rim, short neck, sloping shoulder, round belly and ring foot with the date mark "Made in Guangxu Era, Great Qing" in regular script. Interestingly, on the shoulder of this jar are the five characters "Tianxia Diyi Quan" (Number One Spring in the World) written in seal script and on its belly is the full-text of Emperor Qianlong's poem "Rhapsody for the Number One Spring" written in regular script of the Academic Style. Some collectors suggested that this jar was made for drinking water of the Empress Dowager Cixi, and the water contained by it was shipped daily from Yuquan Shan Hill west of Beijing. Of course, this is only a modern speculation based on the records, but it added a little legend to this porcelain.

Guangxu porcelains survive in the world in large quantity, in recent years, the ones fo which appearing in the auctions are also increasing; according to the author's in complete statistics, only in the mainland art market, there have been over a dozen of Guangxu porcelains sold at closing prices over one million CNY, most of which emerged in the last two years. Some collectors think that after the Jiaqing and Daoguang, it would be easy for the Guangxu porcelains to form subject collections because of the large surviving amounts, so in the future it will become a potential hot spot of the collections of the official kiln products of the late Qing porcelains. In 2010, three Guangxu official kiln products have been sold at prices over one million CNY in Beijing art markets, all of which are in larger sizes. On the of Beijing Poly

Figure 14, Xuantong, Qing, the Blue-and-white Yuhuchun Vase with Bamboo, Rockery and Banana Tree Designs.

Autumn Auction, a pair of 140 cm-high imperial yellow-ground famille-rose floor vases with "Myriad of Birds Hailing the Phoenix" motif created a new record of hammer price which was 2.464 million CNY. They had been collected by Ye Yiquan, who was the son of Ye Chengzhong, a famous businessman in the Minguo Period, and then transferred to Shanghai Friendship Store. On the Spring Auction of the same company, a six-panel screen inlayed with imitation cloisonné enamel porcelain plaques bearing the "Twenty-four Paragons of Filial Piety" motifs was sold at the hammer price of 1.0976 million CNY. On the Autumn Auction of Beijing Hanhai Auction Company, a Guangxu yellow-ground porcelain plate with "Chuxiu Hall" seal mark and Cloud-and-dragon motif was sold at the hammer price of 1.12 million CNY. In recent years, the prices of the finer Guangxu porcelains are mostly around 600 to 700 thousand CNY or so.

The Xuantong Era lasted for only three years and then the emperor Puyi was dethroned while the feudal Qing Dynasty came to an end, so in the past, some people thought that the porcelains made in these three years were not only in small quantities but also in poor qualities. However, according to ceramic experts, it is not the case. Seen from the archives, in the first and second years of Xuantong Era, a lot of porcelains were baked: "In the first year of Xuantong Era, 8,594 pieces of first-class porcelain wares, both wheel-made and model-made, were baked. 18,002 pieces of second-class porcelain wares, both wheel-made and model-made, were baked. 5,745 pieces of porcelain wares were discarded. The reimbursed expenses on the making of these wares were totally 19803.945 teals of silver. In the second year of Xuantong Era, 2,066 pieces of first-class porcelain wares, both wheel-made and model-made, were baked. 5,150 pieces of second-class porcelain wares, both wheel-made and model-made, were baked. 1,740 pieces of porcelain wares were discarded. The reimbursed expenses on the making of these wares were totally 10990.086 teals of silver. Because the archives about the porcelain production in the third year of Xuantong Era are not available, we cannot get the total sum of the porcelains made by the official kiln in the whole Xuantong Era. However, only by the data of the first two years, the official kiln produced more than 40,000 pieces of porcelains.

Currently on the art markets, the prices of Xuantong porcelains are still in the trough, but the performance was impressive in 2010, during which on the mainland auction market, a dozen or so Xuantong porcelains were sold at closing prices of more than 300 thousand CNY each piece, both the quantity and prices of which created new records. On the Spring Auction of Hong Kong Christie's, a famille-rose vase with "Magu Presenting Longevity" motif (Figure 12), which had been collected in Yangzhi Tang and Jingyi Tang, was sold at 1.22 million HKD, which is the highest unit price of Xuantong porcelain so far in art markets. On the Autumn Auction of the same company, a Xuantong blue-and-white bowl with rouge-red "Eight Immortals Crossing the Sea" motif was sold at the price of 0.92 million HKD. The porcelain bowls, awarding vases and Yuhuchun vase bearing the six-character date mark "Made in Xuantong Era, Great Qing" usually seen on the art markets are mainly the famille-rose, polychrome and blue-and-white wares. As early as in 2000, on the Spring Auction of Beijing Hanhai Auction Company, a famille-rose Yuhuchun vase with floral designs (Figure 13) has been sold at the hammer price as high as 225.5 thousand CNY. On the 2005 Autumn Auction of the same company, a blue-and-white Yuhuchun vase with bamboo, rockery and banana tree designs (Figure 14) was sold at the closing price of 418 thousand CNY.

If we see the markets of all of the Qing porcelains as a plate, it can be seen that the prices of Yongzheng and Qianlong porcelains has reached a considerable height, which the common collectors cannot afford; then as the soaring of the prices of Jiaqing porcelains, the prices of the mid and late Qing porcelains on the art market will be rising dramatically, and the future of this plate will be noticeable.

◈ 后 记

　　《帝国余晖——中古陶藏晚清官窑瓷器》一书出版之际，我怀着一颗无比感恩的心写下了这篇后记。本书的出版既是文物艺术品行业浓浓的师情友谊的见证，也包含了我对这个行业的美好祈望，更是对一直以来守望、支持和帮助我们的藏家和友人的一次答谢。文物艺术品是历史文化的遗存和见证，是一段段的文明进程在时光的变迁之后静默的言语，而它所经历的那段时光，正是我们民族风雨前行的辉煌过往，能与它们相伴，因之亲近历史文明的血脉，我的内心充满了感恩和敬畏。要出一本书，一本经过中古陶"双轨制"鉴定为真品、中古陶收藏的瓷器藏品集，是我一直以来的梦想。中陶、中古陶科技鉴定实力的增强，德艺双馨眼学专家队伍的不断扩大，使双轨制鉴定在实践中不断得到肯定，从而加快了我出书梦的实现步伐。

　　今天呈现在读者面前的这一组清晚期官窑瓷器，是中古陶九年来在苏富比、佳士得、嘉德、翰海、保利等拍卖行和中外资深藏家手中陆续购得的，有着很好的传承。这次结集出版，是中古陶经济实力的一次展示，是中古陶"双轨制"鉴定实力的印证，是中古陶"集真养眼"经营理念的结晶。文物艺术品的经营，首先是对历史文化的经营，也是对世道人心的经营。这一批器物，首先经过了中古陶专家委员会的反复论证，在眼学上排除了各种"存疑"，并且又有科技鉴定的结果作为印证。我们提倡"双轨制"文物艺术品鉴定方法，是要在现有的条件下排除器物为假的可能性，从而尽我们所能，守住文物艺术品经营的那道防线。在这个基础上，我们还要发掘文物艺术品的历史文化属性，在器物中体悟和感受那一段段历史文明的文化气息和文化特征。

　　在赝品充斥古玩市场的时代，在高仿品不断撞击我们收藏者脆弱神经的年代，中古陶把这本真品集献给九年来一直不离不弃关注、支持我们的藏家，一直帮助、厚爱我们的文博界的各位领导，一直全力以赴鼓励、成就我成长的专家和各界至爱亲朋……让这本晚清官窑集成为你们闲暇之余养眼的小书，成为你们床头爱看的精美画册，是我最大的心愿。

　　我在这里，要衷心感谢这些年来指给了我文物艺术品正确的经营道路、启发了我的经营理念的老师们和朋友们。他们的言传和身教，让我学会了对文物艺术品的热爱、真诚和敬畏，让我学会了如何面对这个行业。本书的顺利出版，也得益于他们的帮助和扶持，这本书后记最要浓墨重彩书写的是：感谢八十多岁高龄的文博界泰斗吕济民老先生，在炎炎夏日为本书作序并题词；感谢德高望重的著名陶瓷鉴定专家、故宫博物院研究员叶佩兰先生，为本书撰写专论并题词。酷暑难捱，叶佩兰老师几易其稿，亲自选图，先生的敬业精神让我为之深深感动；感谢著名陶瓷鉴定专家、故宫博物院研究员杨静荣老师，在百忙中应邀担任本书的第一主编，先生早年曾在邯郸烧窑取得的经验、渊博的学识以及故宫工作的丰富经历等都使本书更具有学术价值和可读性；感谢北京市文物鉴定委员会副主任、北京市文物局副研究员张如兰先生，感谢著名陶瓷鉴定专家、首都博物馆文物资源调查征集部主任、研究员王春城老师，感谢著名陶瓷鉴定专家、故宫博物院副研究员陈润民老师，老师们在百忙中为本书题字并提出修改意见，使这本书内容更加充实完美；最后，要感谢我的恩师著名书画鉴定专家、书法家、中古陶艺术总监金鑫大师为本书题写书名并题词；感谢著名玉器鉴定专家、社科院考古所研究员古方老师为本书提供了很好的策划建议；感谢《文物天地》编辑阮富春老师为我们撰写专论。

最后说说我自己。十年前一个偶然的投资机会让我与古玩结了缘，自此一往情深，再也没有停止前行的脚步。在事业的感召下，在高雅的艺术品魅力的吸引下，我放弃了自己原来的专业，全身心的投入了这个古老而又神秘的行业。作为一名企业的管理者，在业务上我给自己提出了一个目标，就是"谈起专业知识的时候，要让内行听起来不外行，外行听起来挺内行"。为了这个目标，我首先向书本学习，不仅大量阅读与瓷器知识相关的书籍，还参加了专业课的系统学习，然后是向身边的陶瓷鉴定大家们学习，这是很好的路径。听君一堂课胜读十年书，专家们毫无保留的把他们的实战经验传授给我，近十年的耳濡目染使我受益匪浅。读万卷书，不如行万里路。除了向书本和专家学习外，那就是向实践学习。为了提高眼力，在我的日志上没有休息日，我把大量的时间都用在了跑市场、去博物馆、参观窑址和与科学家、文博界专家一起检测、研究标本上。经过这么多年的修炼，我的鉴定水平和专业知识向票友的水平迈进了一步，也鉴于此，我才有信心担任本书的第二主编。应该说，本书的出版浸透了我大量的心血，我是一个喜欢厚积薄发的人，没有准备的事我是从来不做的。本书从策划到出版整整用了一年多的时间，我亲自撰写了本书器物说明的第一稿，参与了大量的具体编纂工作。出书的过程是一次学习，更是向广大藏友、各位领导、挚爱亲朋的一次工作汇报。

我们深知，一本文物艺术品的书籍，应该是专业的高度与严谨的态度的完美结合，更是编者对文物艺术品的真诚内心的体现。但由于条件和能力所限，这本书还会有很多不完美的地方，敬请各位前辈、各位专家和读者不吝赐教，我们深表感谢。

2011年4月18日

At the moment of the publishing of *The Last Glow of the Empire: the Porcelains of the Late Qing Official Kiln Collected in Zhonggutao*, I finished this postscript with grateful feeling. The publishing of this book is not only the evidence of the deep friendship among our colleagues in the antique art trade and my good hope to our trade but also a reward to our connoisseurs and colleagues caring, supporting and helping us for the long time past. Antique artworks are the remains and evidences of history and culture and the silent language of the progress of the civilizations after the changes of the times. I have deep feelings of gratitude and awed respect to them when I get intimate with the development route of the civilization and history via them. To publish a catalog of the genuine porcelain masterpieces collected in Zhonggutao which have experienced the ordeal of the dual system authentication has been a cherished desire of mine for many years. The strengthening of the scientific identification of Zhonggutao and the expanding of the team of the visual verification experts with high academic ethics and superb experiences are confirming the dual system of antique artwork authentication with their practices and accelerating the fulfillment of the publishing of this book.

The set of porcelains presented to our readers are the products of the official kiln of the late Qing Dynasty acquired by Zhonggutao in the recent nine years from the Sotheby's, Christie's, Guardian, Hanhai, Poly and other auction houses and collections of the senior connoisseurs at home and abroad, all of which have clear and reliable proveniences. The compiling and publishing of this catalog is a demonstration of the economic strength, an evidence of the "dual system" identification scientific and technical reserves of Zhonggutao, and an embodiment of Zhonggutao's managing philosophy of "Concentrating the Genuine and Nurturing the Eyes". The management of antique artworks is first of all the management of the history and culture, as well as the social morals and virtues. The porcelains cataloged in this book have been tested and appraised by the Committee of Experts of Zhonggutao for several times, excluded all doubts and double-proven by the results of modern scientific verification methods. The reason why we advocate the "dual system" verification methods is that we are doing our best to rule out any possibility for the fakes to sneak into our collection under the present condition and to hold the principle of antique artwork management. On this basis, we are also making efforts to explore the historical and cultural properties of the antique artworks and to experience and realize the tastes and features of the cultural atmospheres and identities of the historic periods in which these artworks were created.

In the time of fakes flooding the antique art market and the high replicas repeatedly impacting our collectors' nerves, Zhonggutao dedicates this catalog of genuine porcelain masterpieces to the collectors taking care of us and helping us without even a moment of ignoring, the leaders of the archaeology and museum fields supporting and loving us, the experts and friends of our trade and all fields......to let this book be your pastime and sedative after the hard work or a bedside book for enjoying the beautiful pictures is my greatest wish.

I would like to thank all of the teachers and friends directing me to the right path of the antique art management and inspiring me the correct managing ideas in the past years. Their oral and practicing instructions made me understand the admiration, faith and awe to the cultural heritages, and learn how to face this cause. The successful publishing of this book also benefited from their help and support. Whom I want to specially appreciate in this postscript are: Mr. Lu Jimin, the eighties-year-old dean of the cultural sector, who wrote the preface and inscription for this book in the torrid summer, Mr. Ye Peilan, the respected famous ceramics expert of the Palace Museum, who wrote a monograph and modified several times for this book and personally selected pictures for our catalog, the professionalism of whom deeply moved me, Mr. Yang Jingrong, the famous ceramics expert of Palace Museum, who is invited as the primary editor of this book taking time from his busy schedule, his rich experience gained from the practice in Handan Kiln in the early years and the Palace Museum and vast knowledge made this book more academically valuable and readable, Mr. Zhang Rulan, the deputy director of Beijing Cultural Relics Appraisal Committee and the associate research fellow of Beijing Municipal Cultural Relics Bureau, Mr. Wang Chuncheng, the famous ceramics expert and the director of Department of Cultural Resources Survey and Acquisition of Capital Museum, Mr. Chen Runmin, the famous ceramics expert and the associate research fellow of the Palace Museum, all of whose advices and amendments enriched and perfected this book. Finally, thanks to Mr. Jin Xin, who is my mentor, the celebrated connoisseur for painting and calligraphy, the general artistic supervisor of Zhonggutao, for writing the title and the inscription for the book, Mr. Gu Fang, the famous jade expert of Chinese Academy of Social Sciences, who provides exceptional planning advice, Mr. Ruan Fuchun, the editor of the journal of *Wenwu Tiandi* (Cultural Relics World), who wrote a monograph for our book, the editors, photographers and all the staff of the Cultural Relics Press for the publishing of this book.

Finally, please let me talk about myself and my career. Ten years ago, an occasional investing chance connected me and the antique art trade. Since then, I could not stop the onward paces. Inspired by the cause and attracted by the charms of the elegant art, I gave up my original profession and threw myself completely into this old and mysterious occupation. As a business manager, I set a professional goal for myself, which is "when talking about the professional knowledge, you should let the experts feel that you are not a layperson and the amateurs feel that you are an expert." To reach this goal, I at first studied from the books, not only a large number of those related to the knowledge about porcelain, but also the systematic studies of the specialized courses, and then I learned from the experts on the porcelain appraising, which I found to be a good path. In China, there is a proverb saying, "listening to a good advice is better than reading ten years of books", and I personally feel that to be true. The experts transferred their practical experience to me without any reservation, and I benefited a great deal from their teachings. Reading ten thousand books is not enough, traveling ten thousand miles is necessary. In addition to reading books and learning from experts, I also concentrated on practical learning. In order to improve my visual identification ability, I changed all holidays into workdays and put a lot of time on observing the markets, visiting museums and kilns or testing the samples with the scientists. After so many years of cultivation, my identifying skill and professional knowledge have risen to a higher level, also in view of this, I have confidence to act as the secondary editor of this book. It should be said that I paid a lot of effort for the publication of this book. I like to start my job on a firm ground, and seldom do anything without complete preparation. From planning to publishing, I took more than one year to prepare for this book. I personally wrote the first draft of the artwork descriptions of this book and involved in a lot of specific work of codification. The procedure of publishing a book is also a process of studying, and this book is also a report to the colleagues of the antique art collection circle, all of the leaders and beloved friends.

We know that a book on antique artwork should be the perfect integration of high professional and serious attitude, and the embodiment of the dedication of the authors and editors to the antique art. However, due to the limitations of our conditions and abilities, this book will have a lot of imperfections. We will be grateful for the instructions and suggestions of the experts, senior connoisseurs and all readers.

责任编辑　王　伟
责任印制　陈　杰
特邀校对　王稼丰

图书在版编目（CIP）数据

帝国余晖 ： 中古陶藏晚清官窑瓷器 /杨静荣，
张崇檀主编. — 北京 ： 文物出版社，2011.9
ISBN 978-7-5010-3272-3

Ⅰ．①帝… Ⅱ．①杨… ②张… Ⅲ．①官窑—
瓷器（考古）—中国—清后期 Ⅳ．①K876.3

中国版本图书馆CIP数据核字(2011)第188571号

帝国余晖——中古陶藏晚清官窑瓷器

主　　编　杨静荣　张崇檀
出版发行　文物出版社
地　　址　北京东直门内北小街2号楼
邮　　编　100007
网　　址　www.wenwu.com
邮　　箱　web@wenwu.com
印　　刷　北京雅昌彩色印刷有限公司
版　　次　2011年9月第1版第1次印刷
开　　本　889×1194毫米　1/16
印　　张　13.5
书　　号　ISBN 978-7-5010-3272-3
定　　价　198.00元